PENGUIN BOOKS

Understanding Company Financial Statements

R. H. Parker was born in North Walsham, Norfolk, in 1932. He read Economics at University College, London, from 1951 to 1954. He then served three years' articles in the City of London before becoming a member of the Institute of Chartered Accountants in England and Wales in 1958. Since then he has practised accounting and taught at universities and business schools in Australia, Britain, France and Nigeria.

He is the author, joint author or editor of numerous books and articles on accounting and finance, including the *Macmillan Dictionary of Accounting* (2nd edition, 1992), *Comparative International Accounting* (5th edition, 1998), *Readings in the Concept and Measurement of Income* (2nd edition, 1986) and *Accounting History: Some British Contributions* (1994).

From 1976 to 1997 R. H. Parker was Professor of Accounting at the University of Exeter. He is now Professor Emeritus. He is a former editor of *Accounting and Business Research*, published by the Institute of Chartered Accountants in England and Wales and a former Professorial Research Fellow of the Institute of Chartered Accountants of Scotland. His main research interests are in the international, comparative and historical aspects of accounting.

Understanding Company Financial Statements

FIFTH EDITION

R. H. Parker

PENGUIN BOOKS

For Theresa and Michael

ACKNOWLEDGEMENTS

For 'The Hardship of Accounting' from *The Poetry of Robert Frost*, edited by
Edward Connery Lathem: to the estate of Robert Frost, Edward Connery Lathem
and to Jonathan Cape Ltd. Copyright 1936 by Robert Frost. Copyright © 1964 by
Lesley Frost Ballantine. Copyright © 1969 by Holt, Rinehart & Winston, Inc.
Reprinted by permission of Holt, Rinehart & Winston, Inc.

PENGUIN BOOKS

Published by the Penguin Group
Penguin Books Ltd, 80 Strand, London WC2R 0RL, England
Penguin Putnam Inc., 375 Hudson Street, New York, New York 10014, USA
Penguin Books Australia Ltd, 250 Camberwell Road, Camberwell, Victoria 3124, Australia
Penguin Books Canada Ltd, 10 Alcorn Avenue, Toronto, Ontario, Canada M4V 3B2
Penguin Books India (P) Ltd, 11 Community Centre, Panchsheel Park, New Delhi – 110 017, India
Penguin Books (NZ) Ltd, Cnr Rosedale and Airborne Roads, Albany, Auckland, New Zealand
Penguin Books (South Africa) (Pty) Ltd, 24 Sturdee Avenue, Rosebank 2196, South Africa

Penguin Books Ltd, Registered Offices: 80 Strand, London WC2R 0RL, England

www.penguin.com

First published 1972
Second Edition 1982
Third Edition 1988
Fourth Edition 1994
Fifth Edition 1999
5

Copyright © R. H. Parker, 1972, 1982, 1988, 1994, 1999

Set in 9.5/12 pt Adobe Minion
Typeset by Rowland Phototypesetting Ltd, Bury St Edmunds, Suffolk
Printed in England by Clays Ltd, St Ives plc

Contents

Preface to the Fifth Edition

An eminent company lawyer once wrote of the published financial statements of companies that 'to the average investor or creditor – "the man on the Clapham omnibus" – they are cryptograms which he is incapable of solving'.* This small book is an attempt to make the task easier. It is written for the general reader and the first-year student, not for my fellow accountants, and does not pretend to be more than an introduction to a difficult subject. No previous knowledge is assumed. The emphasis is on analysis and interpretation rather than accounting techniques. Special attention has been paid to making the language of accounting and finance intelligible to the lay person.

The previous editions of this book were published in 1972, 1982, 1988 and 1994. The fifth edition retains the general approach of these editions, but once again the pace of change has been so fast that much has had to be rewritten.

I am indebted to British Vita PLC for allowing me to reprint its 1997 annual report and its 1998 interim report. I am especially grateful to Professor C. W. Nobes for valuable comments on a previous draft of the manuscript, but any errors and misinterpretations that may remain are, of course, my responsibility.

My thanks also to Julie Shortland for much word processing.

* *Gower's Principles of Modern Company Law*, Stevens, 4th edn, 1979, p. 507.

1 Companies and Their Reports

In sooth a goodly company.

Revd Richard Harris Barham, 'The Jackdaw of Rheims'

PURPOSE AND DESIGN OF THE BOOK

The purpose of this book is to show the reader how to understand, analyse and interpret the reports sent by companies to their shareholders, and more especially the financial statements contained in them. In order to do this, we shall look in detail at the 1997 annual report of the British Vita group. We shall also refer occasionally to British Vita's 1996 and earlier reports and to the reports of other companies.

In this first chapter we survey in general terms the contents of a company annual report and look briefly at the nature and constitution of the limited liability company. Chapter 2 describes the various financial statements and introduces many important financial and accounting concepts. This is a vital chapter, providing the basis for the analysis which appears later in the book. Chapter 3 explains as briefly as possible the nature of company taxation and the function of the auditors. Chapter 4 deals with accounting regulation and accounting concepts. Chapter 5 describes certain tools of analysis. Chapter 6 is concerned with profitability and return on investment, Chapter 7 with liquidity and cash flows, and Chapter 8 with sources of funds and capital structure. Chapter 9 summarizes the whole book.

Finance and accounting are specialist subjects. This does not mean that they need remain incomprehensible to the lay person. It does mean, however, that technical terms cannot entirely be avoided. One cannot, after all, learn to drive a car or play a piano without learning some new words. In order to make the learning process as painless as possible, technical terms are explained as they are introduced or shortly thereafter, and a glossary is provided for reference (Appendix B). It is hoped that some readers will want to know more about finance and accounting after reading this book. For such readers the references given in Chapter 9 should be useful.

CONTENTS OF A COMPANY ANNUAL REPORT

The 1997 annual report and accounts of British Vita PLC are reproduced as Appendix C by kind permission of the company. Cross-references to the report will be given in square brackets throughout this book.

The content of British Vita's report is typical of that of most listed companies. To get some idea of this content, it is worth leafing quickly through it. What is the British Vita's group and what do the member companies of it do? The group's own succinct description of itself [p. 1] is that it is an international leader in the application of science, technology and engineering to the production of specialized polymer, fibre and fabric components for the finishing, transportation, apparel, packaging and engineering industries throughout the world. More detail is given in the Group Profile and Review of Operations pages [pp. 7–12].

British Vita PLC, of Middleton, near Manchester, is the parent company of the group. It controls twenty wholly owned subsidiaries operating in the UK, as well as thirty-two Continental European subsidiaries, in some of which there are minority shareholdings, and two subsidiaries each in the United States and Australia and one in Zimbabwe. The group also has six associated undertakings [pp. 43–4].

Turning back to the beginning of the report, we find first of all the results for 1997 (with comparative figures for 1996) in the form of Financial Highlights; that is, in summarized form [p. 1]. This is followed by the Chairman's Statement [p. 2]. Such a statement, although not required by law, is published by almost all companies listed on the London Stock Exchange. The content varies considerably. That of British Vita for

1997 looks both at the immediate past and at prospects for the future. Research has shown that this is one of the most widely read sections of an annual report, no doubt because it is presented in non-technical language and also, unlike most of the report, deals with the future as well as the past.

Pages 4 and 5 provide a financial review of the year, reporting on, *inter alia*, operating results, cash flow and exchange rates. Page 6 provides a Summary of Financial Data 1993–1997. Pages 8–12 provide a review of operations. This is a valuable section as it provides information on the group's various product lines and operations. Some companies combine the financial review and the review of operations into an operating and financial review.

Pages 14 and 15 provide information about the directors and officers of the company, including potted biographies. The board of directors consists both of executive directors and non-executive directors, with the positions of chairman and chief executive held, as in most but not all listed companies, by different persons. The Directors' Report [pp. 16–19] is, unlike the Chairman's Statement and the operating and financial reviews, a document whose contents are largely, but not wholly, determined by law (there is a summary of the legal requirements in the Glossary). The main topics dealt with in British Vita's 1997 report are profits and dividends, principal activities, going concern, corporate governance, re-appointment of directors, share capital, allotment authority, disapplication of pre-emption rights, declarable interests, creditors payment policy, personnel, donations and auditors. The next two pages cover the report of the Remuneration Committee.

There now follows the most important and, for many, the most difficult section of the report: the financial statements [pp. 22–42]. These consist of a list of accounting policies (see Chapter 4), a consolidated profit and loss account, a statement of total recognized gains and losses, two balance sheets (one for the group and one for the parent company), a group cash flow statement and fifteen pages of detailed notes. All of these will be looked at more closely later. For the moment it is enough to note that the consolidated profit and loss account shows the results of the operations of the British Vita *group of companies* for the year ended 31 December 1997; the group balance sheet shows the financial position of the *group* as at 31 December 1997; the parent balance sheet shows the financial position of the *parent company only* as at 31 December 1997; and the cash flow statement shows the cash flows of the *group* during the year ended 31 December 1997.

Pages 43–4 list the principal subsidiary and associated undertakings with a note of the country of incorporation and principal operation and of each undertaking's product or activities.

Pages 45–7 contain the Directors' and Auditors' Responsibility Statements and the Auditors' Report. These are discussed in Chapter 3.

Pages 48–9 give notice of the annual general meeting of the shareholders of the company. Every company must by law hold such a meeting once a year with an interval of not more than fifteen months between meetings.

The ordinary business of the meeting is very formal:

1. To receive and consider the accounts and the reports of the directors and auditors for the year ended 31 December 1997.
2. To declare a final dividend on the ordinary shares (dividends are recommended by the directors but approved and declared by the shareholders).
3. and 4. To reappoint directors.
5. To reappoint the auditors and authorize the directors to fix their remuneration.

There are also three items of special business.

The final pages of the annual report [pp. 50–51] give the address of its 'registered office' (its official address) and the names and addresses of the group's auditors, registrar and share transfer office, principal bankers, stockbrokers, and financial advisers. It also sets out a financial calendar giving the approximate dates on which a preliminary announcement of results is made, the report and accounts circulated, the annual general meeting held, the interim report circulated, and dividend payments made. Information is also given about shareholdings, share price and personal equity plans (PEPs).

British Vita's 1997 report is typical of the vast majority of company annual reports in that it does not include current cost information (see Chapter 4), a valued added statement (see Chapter 6), or an environmental report.

CORPORATE GOVERNANCE

Listed companies such as British Vita are owned by shareholders, most of whom take no part in the formulation of company strategy or the day-to-day operations of the company. This is delegated to a board of directors. Boards are given considerable freedom in the way companies are run and, except in times of crisis, are subject to very little interference from the shareholders. There is thus a separation of ownership from control. The problems of accountability which arise from this were addressed in three reports on corporate governance which now form what is known as the Combined Code. The code is voluntary but is backed up by a listing requirement of the London Stock Exchange.

British Vita's Directors' Report [pp. 16–19] gives details of how the group is managed. There is a main board and a management board. The former, which consists of both executive and non-executive members, has responsibility for the formulation of corporate strategy, approval of acquisitions and major capital expenditure, and treasury policy. The latter controls day-to-day operations.

The alternative to the British unitary board of directors comprising both executives and non-executives is the two-tier board system found in some Continental European countries in which the executives form a board of management which reports to a supervisory board of non-executives. This system has received little support from British business, mainly because it is thought to imply, as in Germany, worker representation on the supervisory board.

As already noted, details of the membership of British Vita's board of directors in 1997 are given on pp. 14–15 of the report together with potted biographies. The non-executives are of two kinds: those with long experience and knowledge of the British Vita group, and those from outside the group with extensive financial experience.

Details of the directors' remuneration and pension entitlements are given in note 9 [pp. 30–32]. The information to be provided on this is governed by company legislation and is summarized in the Glossary (Appendix B to this book). The amounts are determined by a remuneration committee composed of the Chairman of the Board and all the non-executive directors. Details of directors' shareholdings and share options are given in note 20 [pp. 39–40].

USERS OF PUBLISHED ACCOUNTS

Although published financial statements are formally for shareholders only, they are also of great interest to other users and in practice they are treated as general-purpose financial statements available to all users. These other users include potential investors, employees, loan creditors, financial analysts, business contacts (customers and suppliers), the government and the public. Many users are also likely to be 'stakeholders' in the company. Stakeholders can usefully be classified into primary stakeholders (the shareholders), who have an ownership interest in the company; secondary stakeholders (e.g., loan creditors, employees, business contacts and tax collectors), with a financial but not an ownership interest in the company; and tertiary stakeholders, who have no direct financial interest but who are affected, or believe themselves to be affected, by the way in which the company's resources are managed (e.g., persons affected by pollution caused or allegedly caused by the company's activities). It is British Vita's policy to make its annual report generally available and not to prepare statements specifically aimed at other users, especially as many of its employees are also shareholders. Many companies, however, prepare a special report for the employees (sometimes, but not always, distributed with the annual report). This report may emphasize the value added statement (see Chapters 2 and 6) rather than the profit and loss account, and contain information presented in a simpler and more graphic form. Many other users might benefit from simplified financial statements.

MEMORANDUM AND ARTICLES OF ASSOCIATION

Every company must have both a memorandum of association and articles of association. The main contents of the memorandum are the name of the company, the situation of the registered office, a list of the objects for which the company has been formed and a statement that the liability of the members is limited. The list of objects is important since a company cannot legally do anything which is beyond its powers (*ultra vires*).

In practice the problem is avoided by listing every conceivable (and sometimes inconceivable) object that the company is ever likely to have.

The articles are the internal regulations of the company and usually deal with such matters as the rights of particular classes of shares, transfer of shares, powers and duties of directors, accounts, dividends, reserves and quorums for meetings of shareholders and directors. The Companies Act includes a model set of articles called Table A, which can be adopted in full or in a modified form.

CLASSIFICATION OF COMPANIES

The chief characteristics of a limited liability company are: a corporate personality distinct from that of its owners or shareholders; the limiting of the liability of the shareholders to the amount invested (which is not the case for a sole trader or partnership where personal assets are available to pay business debts); and, in principle at least, a perpetual life: companies are born but they do not have to die of old age.

It was not until 1844 that incorporation became possible other than by the slow and difficult processes of a special Act of Parliament or a Royal Charter. It took another eleven years for incorporation by registration to be linked with limited liability, by the Limited Liability Act 1855. The foundations of modern British company law (and also that of Australia, Canada, New Zealand, South Africa and many other Commonwealth or former Commonwealth countries) were laid in the Companies Act 1862. The law has been continually revised since. At the time of writing, most of the companies legislation in force in Britain is contained in the Companies Act 1985 as amended in 1989. The European Commission's active programme of company law harmonization greatly affected British companies (see the section below on company law and the European Union).

At 31 March 1998 there were about 1,184,900 companies registered in Great Britain of which about 11,900 (1 per cent) were public companies and about 1,173,000 (99 per cent) were private companies. In 1997–8 about 205,300 new companies were registered.*

* Department of Trade and Industry, *Companies in 1997–8*, HMSO, 1998.

To explain the differences between public and private companies it is necessary to look at the ways in which companies can be classified. A public company is one whose memorandum of association states that it is such, whose name ends with the words 'public limited company' or 'plc' (or, optionally, 'ccc' for companies registered in Wales) and which has a minimum authorized and allotted share capital, one quarter at least of which has been paid up. The minimum amount is set at present at £50,000. Any company which is not a public company is a private company. A private company is not permitted to issue shares or debentures to the public.

A public company does not *have* to make a public issue of shares or debentures; it simply has the right to do so. Thus only about 2,000 UK public companies are listed (quoted) on a stock exchange and the division between private and public companies is not the same as that between companies with listed shares and those with unlisted shares. It is a necessary but not a sufficient condition for listing that the company be a public company. British Vita PLC is both a public and a listed company.

The Companies Act 1985 also divides companies into large, medium and small, using as criteria balance sheet total, turnover and the average number of employees. Small and medium companies are exempted from filing certain data with the Registrar of Companies. As noted in Chapter 4, listed companies have the option to send summary financial statements to their shareholders. This option has been taken up only by companies with a very large number of shareholders. British Vita has chosen not to issue such statements. There is no maximum limit to the number of shareholders. At 31 December 1997, for example, BG plc (formerly part of British Gas plc) had 1,252,529 shareholders. British Vita had 3,717 shareholders at 9 March 1998 [p. 51].* Not all shareholders are persons. Table 1.1 gives estimates of percentages of market value of shareholdings by sector of *beneficial* holder. Since shares can be held by a nominee, the beneficial holder is not necessarily the same as the registered holder of a share.

The main features to note are the steady fall in the percentage of shares held by persons and the steady rise in the holdings of what are known as

---

* The distinction between shareholders and stockholders, and between shares and stock, is not of practical importance. The terms are increasingly used interchangeably.

Table 1.1. Ownership of Company Shares

	1969 %	1975 %	1981 %	1989 %
Persons	47.4	37.5	28.2	21.3
Charities	2.1	2.3	2.2	2.0
Banks	1.7	0.7	0.3	0.9
Insurance companies	12.2	15.9	20.5	18.4
Pension funds	9.0	16.8	26.7	30.4
Unit trusts	2.9	4.1	3.6	5.9
Investment trusts and other financial institutions	10.1	10.5	6.8	3.2
Industrial and commercial companies	5.4	3.0	5.1	3.6
Public sector	2.6	3.6	3.0	2.0
Overseas sector	6.6	5.6	3.6	12.4
	100.0	100.0	100.0	100.0

Source. The Stock Exchange Survey of Share Ownership, Table 2.1b: Share Register Survey Report End 1989, HMSO, 1991.

institutional shareholders (in particular pension funds but also insurance companies, investment trusts, unit trusts and banks). Overseas holdings of British shares increased significantly in the 1980s.

Some companies, including British Vita, voluntarily disclose shareholder statistics. These may sometimes be difficult to interpret because of the existence of nominee shareholdings. At 9 March 1998 British Vita's shareholders held in total 221,693,950 shares so that the *average* holding was 59,643 shares. The average non-private shareholding, however, was 166,405 shares, whereas the average private shareholding was 7,545 shares. Less than one-third of the shareholders were non-private but they held over 91 per cent of the shares. Shareholdings of 3 per cent or over must be declared to a company by law. British Vita reports [p. 18] that shareholdings of this magnitude were held by the Norwich Union Insurance Society, FMR Corporation/Fidelity International Ltd, Sun Life of Canada, the Prudential Corporation, and the Co-operative Insurance Society Ltd.

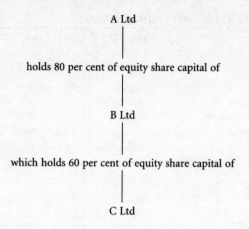

A Ltd

holds 80 per cent of equity share capital of

B Ltd

which holds 60 per cent of equity share capital of

C Ltd

The dominant form of business enterprise in the UK is not the individual undertaking but a group of undertakings (most but not necessarily all of which are companies) headed by what is known as a 'parent undertaking' which controls 'subsidiary undertakings' and has a participating interest in and significantly influences 'associated undertakings'. Associates are distinguished from 'joint ventures' which are controlled jointly by two or more companies. It is possible for a subsidiary itself to have subsidiaries. These are the sub-subsidiaries of the first parent undertaking. In the illustration, A Ltd is the parent, B Ltd its subsidiary, and C Ltd its sub-subsidiary. Note that although A Ltd controls C Ltd, its interest in its shares is only 48 per cent; that is, 80 per cent of 60 per cent. Some parent undertakings exist purely to hold shares in operating subsidiaries. Others, like British Vita PLC, are operating companies as well.

The parent–subsidiary relationship is very common and practically all the annual reports which the reader is likely to be interested in will be those of *groups* of companies. It is possible for subsidiaries to hold shares in each other, but the Companies Act makes it illegal, with minor exceptions, for a subsidiary to hold shares in its parent company.

The annual reports with which we shall be concerned, then, will be those of groups or subgroups of companies. The parent company will usually be a public one. Other members of the group will be British public or private companies or companies incorporated overseas.* All those

* The American equivalent of plc and Ltd is Inc. (i.e., incorporated). The nearest French, German and Dutch equivalents to a British public company are a *société anonyme* (SA), an

concerned are likely to have share capital. It is worth noting in passing that not all companies do have share capital. Some are 'limited by guarantee' (i.e., the members have undertaken to contribute a fixed amount to the assets of the company in the event of its being wound up). The London School of Economics and Political Science is an example. Some companies are even unlimited; since these have the privilege of not publishing their accounts, they are not relevant to this book. They are used by professionals who desire corporate form but are not permitted to limit their liability, or by those who value the privilege of non-disclosure more than the limitation of liability (e.g., the C&A department store). They have become more important since the Companies Act 1967 abolished 'exempt private companies' (essentially family companies exempt from publishing their accounts).

COMPANY LAW AND THE EUROPEAN UNION

Most amendments to British company law from 1980 onwards are the result of implementing the company law 'directives' of the EU. Directives form part of UK law only when they have been incorporated into our domestic legislation. The most important directives so far as company financial reporting is concerned have been the fourth (on the accounts of individual companies), the seventh (on the accounts of groups) and the eighth (on auditors). It was the fourth directive that introduced into UK legislation standardized formats for financial statements (see Chapter 4) and a three-tier classification into large, medium and small companies.

INTERIM REPORTS

Twelve months is a long time to wait for information about the details of the financial progress of a company. It has therefore become increasingly common for major companies to issue unaudited interim reports

Aktiengesellschaft (AG) and a *Naamloze Vennootschap* (NV); to our private companies, *société à responsabilité limitée* (SARL), *Gesellschaft mit beschränkter Haftung* (GmbH) and *Besloten Vennootschap* (BV).

at half-yearly and sometimes quarterly intervals. Listed companies are required by the Stock Exchange to circularize (or insert as a paid advertisement in two leading daily newspapers) a half-yearly interim report to shareholders not later than six months from the date of the notice calling an annual general meeting.

British Vita's interim report for the six months ended 30 June 1998 is reproduced in Appendix D. It comprises a chairman's statement, a consolidated profit and loss account, a group balance sheet, a cash flow statement, a segmental analysis of turnover and operating profit and a page of notes. Interim reports give much less information than annual reports but they have grown in size in recent years.

It is, however, with the annual financial statements that this book is mainly concerned. Now that we have sufficient background information, they can be looked at in more detail.

The Financial Statements

The statements was interesting but tough.

Mark Twain, *The Adventures of Huckleberry Finn*, Chapter 17

ASSETS, LIABILITIES AND SHAREHOLDERS' FUNDS

At the core of any company's annual report are the financial statements. Those for the British Vita group for the year ended 31 December 1997 are reproduced in Appendix C. We shall start by discussing the 1997 group balance sheet (the column of figures furthest to the left on p. 26 of the appendix). This is a statement of the financial position of British Vita and its subsidiaries at 31 December 1997 as if they were one company.

Before 1981, British companies had the right to present a balance sheet in any way they pleased, so long as certain items were disclosed either on the face of the balance sheet or in the notes. As a result of the EU's fourth directive on company accounts, balance sheets are now more standardized in form (see Chapter 4). All company balance sheets, however, are built up from three main categories; namely, assets, liabilities and shareholders' funds. Assets can be defined as rights or other access to future economic benefits controlled by a company as a result of past transactions or other events. In most cases, but not all, control derives from legal ownership. Liabilities can be defined as the obligations of a company to transfer economic benefits as a result of past transactions or other events. The relationship between the assets, liabilities and shareholders' funds can be looked at either from the point of view of shareholders (a 'proprietary' approach) or from the point of view of the company as a whole (an 'entity' approach). Two forms of the fundamental balance sheet identity can thus be derived:

Proprietary: assets – liabilities = shareholders' funds
Entity: assets = shareholders' funds + liabilities.

Very broadly, all that is being said is that, firstly, what a company owns *less* what a company owes is equal to the value of the shareholders' funds invested in it and that, secondly, what a company owns is financed partly by the owners (the shareholders) and partly by outsiders (the liabilities). Either way, a balance sheet must, by definition, balance. The useful accounting technique known as double entry ('debits' and 'credits') is based on these same identities (see Appendix A).

As we shall see in the next few sections, the three categories can each be subdivided: for example, shareholders' funds can be divided into share capital and reserves; assets into fixed assets and current assets; and liabilities into current liabilities (i.e., creditors falling due within one year), creditors falling due after more than one year, and provisions for liabilities and charges.

British Vita has adopted a proprietary approach and presents its consolidated balance sheet in the form shown on p. 15, opposite (see also Appendix C, p. 26). Broadly, the capital and reserves are represented by the sum of the total assets less current liabilities, creditors falling due after more than one year and the provisions for liabilities and charges. Minority interests represent the proportion of the subsidiaries' assets and liabilities which are owned by outside shareholders. The same data is presented rather differently in the Summary of Financial Data [p. 6]: the fixed assets figure is split into tangible fixed assets (£225.8 million) and investments (£18.8 million); and the sum of the net current assets, creditors (amount falling due after one year) and provisions for liabilities and charges (£42.6 million) is split between net working capital (£34.6 million) and net cash (£8.0 million).

The second important financial statement is the consolidated profit and loss account [p. 24]. While a balance sheet represents the financial position at a particular point in time, a profit and loss account (the American phrase is income statement) relates to a period, in this case the year ended 31 December 1997. It shows, from the point of view of the shareholders, the results of the year's activities. The British Vita group made sales (turnover) in 1997 of £808.4 million. The operating profit was £55.5 million; after addition of the share of profit of associated undertakings and net interest receivable, this figure rose to £66.2 million (profit on ordinary activities before taxation). This was reduced by taxation to £44 million (profit on ordinary activities after taxation). After allowing for minority interests the profit for the year available for the shareholders came to £43.8 million. Out of this amount, dividends have been or will be paid to the shareholders, amounting altogether to £19.4 million. This leaves £24.4 million to be retained (ploughed back).

	£m
Fixed assets	244.6
Current assets	296.6
Creditors: amounts falling due within one year	(200.9)
Net current assets	95.7
Total assets less current liabilities	340.3
Creditors: amounts falling due after more than one year	(34.4)
Provisions for liabilities and charges	(18.7)
	287.2
Capital and reserves	286.1
Minority interests	1.1
	287.2

The group profit and loss account is drawn up from the point of view of the shareholders in the parent company. A rather different view of the same figures can be gained by preparing a statement of value added. Unlike the balance sheet and the profit and loss account, this statement is not required by law. The philosophy behind it is that the group by its activities creates new wealth ('adds value'), which is then shared out among the employees, the providers of capital and the government, with a balance being retained to provide for the maintenance and expansion of assets.

Although British Vita, like most other companies, no longer publishes a statement of value added, it is possible to derive one so long as wages and salaries are disclosed. The necessary calculations are shown in Chapter 6. The statement given there demonstrates that value added was applied in 1997 as follows:

	%
Employees	65
Providers of capital:	
interest	1
dividends to British Vita shareholders	7
minority shareholders	0
Governments (as taxation)	8
Retentions for replacement and expansion:	
depreciation	10
retained profit	9
	100

It is worth looking more closely at the link between the profit and loss account and the balance sheet. How can a company grow – that is, how can it increase its assets? Look again at the identity:

assets = liabilities + shareholders' funds.

It is clear that the only ways to increase the assets are to increase the liabilities (to borrow) or to increase the shareholders' funds. How can a company increase the latter? There are two possibilities: it can issue more shares or it can plough back profits (assuming, of course, that it is making some). Ploughing back profits is the simplest but not necessarily the cheapest source of long-term finance for a company. Also, the more a company ploughs back, the less, in the short run at least, there will be available for paying dividends. The recorded amount of both assets and shareholders' funds can also be increased by a revaluation of the former (see the section below on tangible fixed assets).

The inflows and outflows of cash into a company are disclosed not in the balance sheet or profit and loss account but in a cash flow statement. In 1997 the British Vita group [p. 27] generated a net cash inflow from operating activities of £74 million. Since, as will be stressed in Chapter 7, increasing cash and making profits are not the same, this figure differs considerably from the operating profit of £55 million. A reconciliation is provided in note 24 [p. 42]. After allowing for net cash inflows from returns on investments and servicing of finance, and cash outflows relating to taxation, capital expenditure, acquisitions and disposals, and equity dividends paid, the net cash inflow was reduced to a negative £10.3 million. Adding to this the cash outflows and inflows related to the management of liquid resources and financing (mainly the issue of loans and ordinary shares), the result was a decrease in cash during the year of £2.8 million.

All three statements are linked to each other. The retained profit for the year forms part of the profit and loss account item in the balance sheet [see note 21, p. 41]. The decrease in cash is related to the movement during the year in the cash at bank and short-term investments item in the balance sheet [see note 25, p. 42].

CURRENT ASSETS, CURRENT LIABILITIES AND WORKING CAPITAL

Current assets comprise those assets which are not intended for continuing use in the business. They consist mainly of cash, debtors and stocks. The British Vita group at 31 December 1997 had current assets valued at £296.6 million, comprising stocks ('inventories' in US terminology) of £75.1 million, debtors ('accounts receivable') of £161.5 million and cash at bank and short-term investments of £60 million. The figure for stocks may vary according to the rules of valuation adopted. British Vita's policy is set out as follows [p. 22]:

Stocks are valued at the lower of first-in, first-out cost and net realisable value; cost includes appropriate production overhead expenses.

The use of the lower of cost or net realizable value (i.e., expected selling price net of selling expenses) is standard practice in Britain. The phrase 'first-in, first-out' (FIFO) refers to the assumption that the stocks acquired first have been sold or used up first. An alternative assumption, last-in, first-out (LIFO), is popular in the USA but rare in Britain. The cost of finished goods includes not only raw materials and direct labour but also production overheads (but not administrative or distribution overheads). In note 13 [p. 35] the group's stocks are analysed into raw materials and consumable stores on the one hand (57 per cent) and work in progress and finished goods (43 per cent) on the other. These percentages reflect the bulkiness of the finished products, stocks of which, especially in the parent company, are kept at a minimum.

The debtors figure is usually net of an allowance (or provision) for doubtful debts. Cash at bank may be thought to present no problem of valuation, but where it is held overseas and exchange rates are volatile, or the foreign currency cannot easily be remitted, its value in sterling may be uncertain. The general problem of foreign currency accounting is discussed further in Chapter 4.

Current liabilities are also described in the group balance sheet as 'creditors: amounts falling due within one year'. The group's current liabilities of £200.9 million at 31 December 1997 are analysed in note 16 [p. 36]. The most important are trade creditors (i.e., amounts owing to suppliers) of £99.6 million, accruals and deferred income of £25.4 million, corporation tax of £17.6 million, other taxes and social security costs of £13.2 million and the proposed dividend of £10 million. Net current assets are also referred to as net working capital, or (more usually) just working capital. The relationship between current assets and current liabilities is very important and is discussed in Chapter 7 on liquidity.

FIXED ASSETS

Fixed assets comprise those assets which are intended for use on a continuing basis for the purpose of the company's activities. Stocks, for example, are not regarded as fixed assets since they are acquired either for immediate resale (e.g., cigarettes, as sold by a tobacconist) or as raw materials for use in manufacturing operations, or are the finished or partly finished ('work in progress') results of such operations. It is the intention of the directors that determines whether an asset is fixed or not. Plant and vehicles, for example, are the *current* assets of a company whose business it is to manufacture them for sale.

It will be seen from the group balance sheet and notes 11 and 12 [pp. 33–5] that the net book values of the fixed assets of the British Vita group at 31 December 1997 were as follows:

	£m	£m
Tangible fixed assets:		
land and buildings	115.3	
plant and vehicles	110.5	
		225.8
Investments in:		
listed associated undertakings	9.6	
unlisted associated undertakings	7.5	
other investments	1.7	
		18.8
Total		244.6

TANGIBLE FIXED ASSETS

British Vita's fixed assets are thus of two kinds: tangible fixed assets and investments. Note 11 [p. 33] reveals that the plant and vehicles are shown at cost and the land and buildings at a valuation made in 1996 with additions since at cost. 'Cost' in accounting has usually meant the historical cost of acquisition or manufacture (if the asset was made by the company for its own use). Historical cost has been favoured by accountants because it is thought to be objective and verifiable by an independent third party such as an auditor. It can, however, get seriously out of line with current market values, especially in times of inflation. British Vita discloses that, had their land and buildings not been revalued, they would have been stated in the group balance sheet at a net book value of £100.7 million instead of £115.3 million.

In accordance with the Companies Act, British Vita provides a breakdown of its land and buildings into freehold, long leasehold and buildings subject to finance leases.

DEPRECIATION

The concept of depreciation means different things to different people, but in an accounting context it normally means spreading the net cost (sometimes after adjustment or revaluation) of a fixed asset over its estimated useful economic life. British Vita explains its policy as follows [pp. 22–3]:

Depreciation of tangible fixed assets is provided at rates estimated to write off the cost or valuation of assets over their useful lives, the principal rates of annual straight line depreciation being:
(a) Freehold buildings 2.5%. Freehold land is not depreciated.
(b) Leasehold land and buildings 2.5% or over the period of the lease if less than forty years.
(c) Plant between 10% and 33.33%.
(d) Vehicles between 16% and 25%.

British Vita thus uses the straight line method of depreciation. Under this method the cost less estimated scrap value of a fixed asset is divided by the number of years of its estimated useful life. If, for example, a machine costs £1,200 and is expected to have a scrap value of £130 at the end of an estimated useful life of ten years, the annual depreciation using this method will be £1,070 ÷ 10 = £107.

Less popular but still sometimes found in Britain is the reducing balance method of depreciation. As the name implies, the amount of depreciation charged each year under this method decreases over the life of the asset. If, for example, a rate of 20 per cent were chosen for the asset which costs £1,200, the annual depreciation charges would be calculated as shown on p. 21.

The machine has been written down to its approximate scrap value. The correct percentage can be found by trial and error or by use of the formula:

$$1 - n\sqrt{\frac{s}{c}}$$

where n is the number of years, s the estimated scrap value and c the cost. In this case:

$$1 - 10\sqrt{\frac{130}{1200}} = 0.2.$$

The charging of depreciation simultaneously reduces the recorded amount of the fixed asset and reduces net profit.

For the year ended 31 December 1997 the group charged against profits

£27.3 million of depreciation [note 3, p. 29]. The amounts given for the fixed assets in the group balance sheet are net of all accumulated depreciation, not only that of the current year but of all previous years since the purchase of the assets concerned.

		£
Cost		1,200
Year 1	Depreciation 20% of £1,200	240
		960
Year 2	Depreciation 20% of £960	192
		768
Year 3	Depreciation 20% of £768	154
		614
Year 4	Depreciation 20% of £614	123
		491
Year 5	Depreciation 20% of £491	98
		393
Year 6	Depreciation 20% of £393	79
		314
Year 7	Depreciation 20% of £314	63
		251
Year 8	Depreciation 20% of £251	50
		201
Year 9	Depreciation 20% of £201	40
		161
Year 10	Depreciation 20% of £161	32
		129

FIXED ASSET INVESTMENTS

British Vita has a substantial investment in associated undertakings [p. 34]. As explained in Chapter 1, these are companies or other enterprises that are not controlled but are significantly influenced. For example, British Vita may have the right to appoint members of their boards of directors.

The shares of these associates are valued in the company's own accounts at cost less amounts written off, but this is increased in the *group* balance sheet to include a proportionate share of their reserves (retained profits) since acquisition. This accounting treatment, which differs from that used for a subsidiary, is known as the 'equity method'. It is also known as one-line consolidation.

As for associated companies, the shares of subsidiaries in a *parent company* balance sheet are valued at cost less amounts written off. The shares of most subsidiaries, however, are eliminated from group balance sheets and replaced by their underlying assets and liabilities. Subsidiaries may be excluded from consolidation if their inclusion would not make a material difference or would cause disproportionate expense or undue delay. In rare circumstances they must be excluded. When so excluded, their shares are nevertheless included as investments, valued at cost less amounts written off.

INTANGIBLE FIXED ASSETS

A third category of fixed asset, which is not represented in British Vita's balance sheet, is the intangible fixed asset. This is a non-monetary fixed asset which is without physical substance. Some intangibles – for example, patents, trade marks and copyrights – can be separately identified and may be extremely valuable. The music publishing copyrights of the EMI Group, for instance, are carried in its 1998 balance sheet at £529.1 million and account for well over half its fixed assets.

Goodwill is the term used for intangible assets which cannot be separately identified. A company is not just a collection of tangible assets. It is, or should be, a going concern whose total value, by reason of its proven ability to earn profits, is greater than the sum of its parts. It is the difference between the total value and the sum of the parts (including identifiable intangibles) which constitutes goodwill. It should not be regarded as in any way a fictitious asset: to be valuable, an asset does not have to be tangible. Goodwill is, however, very difficult to value objectively and company law does not permit it to appear in a balance sheet unless it has been purchased, and even then it usually has been written off either immediately or quite quickly. 'Goodwill arising on consolidation' (goodwill on acquisition) represents the excess of the cost of shares in subsidiary companies over the fair value of their net tangible and identifiable intangible assets at the date of acquisition; that is, the parent company was willing to pay more to purchase a company than the sum of its tangible and identifiable intangible fixed and net current assets. British Vita in 1997 wrote off goodwill on acquisition to reserves [p. 22, para. 2]. The cumulative amount of goodwill resulting from acquisitions and investments in associated undertakings in 1997 and earlier financial years amounts to £23.1 million [note 21, p. 41]. The accounting rules for goodwill and other intangibles were changed in 1997. Goodwill on acquisition arising in 1998 onwards is not to be written off to reserves, as is shown in the consolidated profit and loss account and group balance sheet in British Vita's interim report [Appendix D].

LOANS AND OTHER BORROWINGS

The item 'Creditors: amounts falling due after more than one year' in British Vita's group balance sheet represents the extent to which the group, not wishing to obtain further long-term funds from its shareholders, has borrowed from outsiders, both in the UK and overseas. Details are given in notes 17 and 18 [pp. 37–8]. The major part consists of loans both long-term (not wholly repayable within five years) and medium-term (repayable within five years). The proportion of the loans payable within one year is included under the heading 'Creditors: amounts falling due within one year'.

Banks are an obvious source of outside finance and most of British Vita's borrowings are in the form of bank loans. These are not the only forms of borrowing. A 'debenture' is a document providing evidence of a long-term borrowing or loan. Debentures are usually, but not necessarily, secured on the assets of the company, in which case they may be known as mortgage debentures. If a company fails in its obligation to pay interest or repay the loan, the secured property of the company can be sold in order to provide the necessary funds. The phrase 'unsecured debenture' is unusual, 'unsecured loan' often being preferred. The term 'debenture stock' is used when a company instead of issuing individual debentures has created one loan fund to be divided among a class of lenders, each of whom will receive a debenture stock certificate. Companies may, and often do, make more than one issue of debentures, the terms of issue and, in particular, the rate of interest varying according to the financial circumstances of the time. Such issues may be made at par (i.e., at face value), at a discount (less than face value) or at a premium (more than face value). Issue at a discount increases the effective interest rate payable; issue at a premium (which is rare) reduces it. Issues are often made at a discount in order to keep the interest rate on the par value (known as the coupon rate) a reasonably round figure, while allowing the effective rate to be adjusted more finely.

Debentures and loans may be secured by a fixed charge on a particular asset or by a floating charge on all the assets or particular classes of asset. A floating charge, unlike a fixed charge, allows a company to dispose of the assets charged in the usual course of business without obtaining special permission from the lender. Stock-in-trade is a particularly suitable asset to be charged in this manner. If assets are, or may be, used as security for more than one loan, it is necessary to state the order of priority of the lenders (for example, debenture stock may be stated to be secured by a *first* floating charge).

Some debentures are irredeemable – that is, they will never have to be repaid (unless the company is wound up) – but most are redeemable. It is common not only to specify the latest date, but also to give the company the power to redeem earlier if it so wishes. This is especially useful if debentures are issued in times of high interest rates and if there is an expectation of lower rates later.

In principle there is a clear distinction between borrowings and share-holders' funds. In practice, especially in recent years, the distinction has become blurred by the issue by some companies of 'hybrid' securities – securities with the characteristics of both debt and equity. There has also been an increase in 'off balance sheet finance'; that is, borrowing in such a fashion that the debt does not appear as a balance sheet item. Standard accounting practice does not permit the exclusion from the balance sheet of finance leases, which are long-term contracts allowing the company the use, but not the ownership, of an asset in return for a periodic rental. British Vita includes finance leases as part of its borrowings [note 17, p. 37]. Both leasing and off balance sheet financing are discussed further in Chapter 8.

How much to borrow, and when and in what form to do so are

vital matters to any company. We shall look at these problems in Chapter 8.

PROVISIONS FOR LIABILITIES AND CHARGES

Provisions for liabilities and charges are defined as amounts retained as reasonably necessary for the purpose of providing for any liability or loss which is either likely to be incurred or certain to be incurred, but uncertain as to the amount or as to the date on which it will arise. The two most important provisions of this kind, as British Vita's note 19 [p. 38] demonstrates, are for deferred taxation and for pensions. Deferred taxation is discussed in Chapter 3. Most companies provide pension benefits for their employees. British Vita's pension arrangements are set out at length in note 10 [p. 32].

In 1998, an accounting standard (FRS 12) was issued which tightened up the definition of 'provision'. A provision must now involve an obligation to a third party. For example, a provision for the costs of a reorganization or redundancies could not be made merely because the directors expect to incur such costs in the future.

SHARE CAPITAL AND RESERVES

The shareholders' funds section of the group balance sheet is subdivided into share capital and reserves. Further details are given in notes 20 and 21 [pp. 39–41].

Shareholders differ from debenture-holders in three main ways: they are members (owners) of the company, not lenders; they receive dividends (a share of the profits), not interest; and, except in special circumstances, the cost of their shares will not be repaid (redeemed) to them by their company. Listed shares can of course be sold to other investors on a stock exchange, but both the redemption of shares and the buying by a company of its own shares, although allowable subject to certain restrictions, are relatively uncommon in the UK.

There are two main types of shares: ordinary and preference. The difference between an ordinary shareholder and a preference shareholder is very important. The latter is usually entitled only to a dividend at fixed rate (4.2 per cent in the case of British Vita which bought back and cancelled its preference shares in 1997), but has priority of repayment in the event of the company being wound up. This is not always so, however, and the exact rights must always be looked up in the company's articles of association. Preference shares may be cumulative or non-cumulative. British Vita's were cumulative, which means that if the company misses a dividend payment it carries it forward to the next year. Any arrears of preference dividends must be disclosed. Non-cumulative preference dividends, on the other hand, do not have to be carried forward.

The size of the dividends paid to ordinary shareholders varies according to the profits made by the company. It can be seen from note 7 [p. 30] that British Vita paid an interim ordinary dividend of 4.25 p per share during 1997 and that a final ordinary dividend of 4.5 p is proposed. The total ordinary dividend is thus 8.75 p. The par or face value of the ordinary shares is 25 p each [p. 39, note 20], and the total dividend could be described as a dividend of 35 per cent on the par value.

More important to an investor is the relationship between the dividend and the current *market* price of the share. This is known as the dividend yield and is discussed in Chapter 8 in the context of earning yields and price–earnings ratios. For the moment, it should be noted that every share must have a par value* but that this is not necessarily the same as the issue price of the shares or their market price. Shares can be issued at more than their par value: this gives rise to a share premium. The British Vita group has a share premium of £92 million [p. 41, note 21]. A share premium cannot be distributed, but it can be used to make a bonus or capitalization issue (see p. 99). Once a share has been issued, its market price fluctuates from day to day in accordance with supply and demand. If the shares can be bought and sold on a stock exchange, then the current market price can easily be found in the financial pages of a newspaper or from the *Stock Exchange Daily Official List*. The most complete newspaper list is given in the *Financial Times*. The information given in that paper's daily share information service is further discussed in Chapter 8.

A company does not have to issue all its shares at once, nor does it have to request full payment on the shares immediately. British Vita has

---

* No-par-value shares are common in North America but illegal in the UK.

authority to issue (i.e., it has authorized capital of) 300 million ordinary shares of 25 p each [p. 39, note 20]. As at 31 December 1997 it had issued 221.7 million ordinary shares (par value £55.4 million). All the shares are described as being fully paid; that is, the company does not have the right to call up any further amounts from the shareholders. They could have been partly paid. For example, a 25 p share could be payable 5 p on application for the shares, a further 5 p on allotment, when the directors decide to whom the shares are going to be issued (or 'allotted'), and the remaining 15 p in calls. Thus, in summary, one can distinguish authorized, issued, called-up and paid-up share capital.

In 1997 British Vita increased its issued ordinary share capital in two ways: by the allotment of 655,168 new shares, fully paid, in accordance with the rules of the employee share option schemes; and by the allotment of 91,366 shares, fully paid, to subscribers to the company's personal equity plans (PEPs).

Details of the group's reserves are given in note 21 [p. 41]. The Companies Act distinguishes for a *company* between 'distributable' and 'undistributable' reserves. The former comprises realized profits less realized losses. British Vita's group profit and loss account balance of £119.9 million is regarded by the company as distributable. The share premium account, revaluation reserve (created as a result of the revaluation of fixed assets on the other side of the balance sheet), and other reserves, totalling altogether £110.8 million, are not so regarded. The movements on reserves during the year included the increase in share premium resulting from the share issues; the increase in the retained profit; and the write-off of goodwill arising on acquisitions.

It is very important not to confuse reserves with cash. To say that a company has large reserves is not the same thing as saying that it has plenty of cash. If a company has reserves it must have net assets of equal amount, but these assets may be of any kind (e.g., machinery, stock-in-trade). Thus it is perfectly possible (and often sensible) for a company to have both large reserves and a large bank overdraft.

CONSOLIDATED PROFIT AND LOSS ACCOUNT

British Vita's consolidated profit and loss account is given on page 24 of its annual report. It follows the most popular of the four formats permitted by the Companies Act (see Chapter 4) and summarizes the year's operations from the point of view of the shareholders.

The first item in the profit and loss account is turnover (£808.4 million). This represents the net amounts invoiced to external customers by companies in the group but excludes value added taxes and sales taxes and the sales of the associated undertakings [p. 22]. Turnover within the group (i.e., between the parent and its subsidiaries) is not included, since to do so would merely inflate both sales and purchases. Note 1 [p. 28] analyses turnover by class of business and by geographical origin and destination.

Cost of sales (£612.1 million) – that is, the cost of the goods sold during 1997 whether or not manufactured in 1997 – is deducted from turnover to give the gross profit (£196.3 million). From this are further deducted distribution costs (£52.1 million) and administrative expenses (£88.7 million) to give an operating profit of £55.5 million. Some of the more important constituents of cost of sales, distribution costs and administrative expenses are disclosed in notes 3 [p. 29] and 9 [pp. 30–32]. From these notes we can discover total employment costs (£181.1 million), broken down into wages and salaries, social security costs and other pension costs, depreciation (£27.3 million) and the cost of operating leases, auditors' remuneration and research and development, plus government grants received.

The next item is the group share of profits of associated undertakings. The accounting treatment of associated undertakings differs, as we have seen, from that of subsidiaries. Like the latter, the appropriate share of profit or loss before tax is brought into the group results – not just the dividends received; but, unlike subsidiaries, it is brought in as one figure, not split into its component parts. This is because the group controls the sales, wages, etc., of its subsidiaries but not those of its associated undertakings. Nevertheless, British Vita discloses in note 4 [p. 29] its share of the turnover of its associated undertakings (£122.9 million), its share of the profits less losses, before and after tax (£9.6 million and £6.2 million respectively), and dividends receivable from them (£1.6 million).

In the balance sheet, it will be remembered, the underlying assets and liabilities of an associated undertaking are *not* brought in (because they are not under British Vita's control), but instead the cost of the original investment is augmented by a share of the associated undertaking's retained profits since acquisition.

The next item is net interest receivable of £1.1 million, further details of which are given in note 5 [p. 29].

It is now possible to calculate profit on ordinary activities before taxation (£66.2 million). Taxation (see Chapter 3) amounts to £22.2 million, so profit on ordinary activities after taxation is £44 million.

The profit after tax is not the same as the profit for the financial year. Two further items may need to be deducted: the share of the profit after tax which is attributable to the minority shareholders in the group (£0.2 million in 1997); and 'extraordinary' items. British Vita records no extraordinary items in its 1997 accounts. Standard accounting practice distinguishes between extraordinary items and exceptional items. *Extraordinary items* are material items possessing a high degree of abnormality which arise from events or transactions that fall outside the ordinary activities of a business and which are not expected to recur. They can be profits or losses; the tax on them is shown separately. This is a very restrictive definition and extraordinary items are seldom, if ever, found in practice. In contrast, *exceptional items* are material items which derive from events or transactions that fall within the ordinary activities of a business and which need to be disclosed by virtue of their size or incidence. They include gains and losses on the sale of fixed assets, which must be shown separately (net of tax) as exceptional items on the face of the profit and loss account.

We have at last reached the profit for the financial year. This amounted to £43.8 million in 1997. The remainder of the profit and loss account is concerned with the distribution or retention of this sum: £19.4 million has been or will be distributed; £24.4 million is to be retained. Details of dividends are given in note 7 [p. 30]. An interim dividend of £9.4 million has already been distributed to the ordinary shareholders. A final dividend of £10 million is proposed.

At the foot of the group profit and loss account a note is given of the earnings per share. Earnings per share (EPS) is based on earnings per *ordinary* share. The relevant figure for earnings was £43.8 million in 1997 – the profit for the financial year. EPS is not of interest to preference shareholders since their dividend is fixed irrespective of the level of earnings. As at 31 December 1997 there were 221.7 million shares [note 20, p. 39]. The EPS calculation is, however, based on the weighted average of ordinary shares in issue during the year; namely, 221.2 million shares [note 8, p. 30]. The calculation of EPS is thus:

$$\text{EPS} = \frac{43,800,000 \times 100}{221,200,000} \text{ p} = 19.8 \text{ p}.$$

The concept of earnings per share is discussed further in Chapter 8.

Profit earned needs to be related to investment made, and compared, if possible, with the performance of similar companies. Profitability and return on investment form the main subjects of Chapter 6.

The consolidated profit and loss account is followed [on p. 25] by a statement of total recognized gains and losses; a note of historical cost profits and losses; and a reconciliation of movements in shareholders' funds. There is also reference to a statement of movements in shareholders' funds.

The purpose of the statement of total recognized gains and losses is to bring together those gains and losses which have been passed through the profit and loss account and those which have not; that is, the profit for the financial year (£43.8 million), the unrealized surplus on revaluation of properties (nil in 1997) and the currency translation differences on foreign currency net investments (– £14.4 million).

The note of historical cost profits and losses (which could have been shown in the notes rather than here) provides a calculation of what British Vita's profit on ordinary activities before taxation and retained profit for the financial year would have been if they had been based entirely on historical cost accounting without any revaluation of fixed assets. It can be seen that the main effect of the revaluations was to increase the depreciation charge so that the reported figures (£66.2 million and £24.4 million) were slightly lower than they otherwise would have been (£67.1 million and £25.3 million). The purpose of the statement is to facilitate inter-company comparisons: not all British companies revalue their assets and those that do may not do so every year or on a comparable basis. It also makes it easier to identify distributable profits, since these depend upon historical cost calculations.

The purpose of the reconciliation of movements in shareholders' funds (which can also be shown as a note) is to explain how the total of shareholders' funds has changed during the year. For many companies in most years, as for British Vita in 1997, the largest item is the retained profit (profit for the financial year less dividends). Shareholders' funds were also increased by new share capital subscribed, other recognized gains and losses (net) and reduced by the write-off of goodwill.

Shareholders' funds are made up of share capital and reserves. A statement of movements in reserves is given in note 21 [p. 41]. From this can be seen how each reserve category (share premium account, revaluation reserve, other reserves, profit and loss account) changed during the year. The most important changes in 1997 were a result of the retention of profit and the write-off of goodwill.

CASH FLOW STATEMENT

A cash flow statement discloses a business's inflows and outflows of cash during an accounting period. In the UK, cash flow statements are required not by company law but by accounting standard (see Chapter 4). They may be prepared by the 'direct method' or the 'indirect method' (see below). Cash flows are classified under the following headings:

> operating activities
> returns on investments and servicing of finance
> taxation
> capital expenditure and financial investments
> acquisitions and disposals
> equity dividends paid
> management of liquid resources
> financing

The statement concludes with the increase (decrease) in cash during the year. Under the indirect method (used by British Vita), the cash flow from operating activities is calculated by adding back to operating profit any depreciation charged and increases/decreases in debtors, creditors and stocks. Details are given in note 24 [p. 42]. The more easily understood but less popular direct method reports, in classified form, the cash receipts and cash payments for each activity. The direct method is more straightforward than the indirect method but it lacks a link with the profit and loss account. By definition cash flow statements exclude non-cash transactions. For this reason, the accounting standard also requires footnote disclosure of major non-cash transactions.

With this background we can now look at the cash flow statement of British Vita for 1997. In summary the cash inflows and outflows of the group in 1997 (arranged in order of importance) were as follows:

	£m
Cash inflows	
Net cash inflow from operating activities	74.0
Net increase in loans	16.3
Interest received	3.4
Issues of ordinary share capital	1.2
Other cash inflows (net of other cash outflows)	1.0
	95.9
Cash outflows	
Capital expenditure	32.9
Acquisitions and disposals	19.9
Dividends paid	18.8
Taxation paid	15.6
Interest paid	1.7
Decrease in liquid resources other than cash	9.8
	98.7
Decrease in cash	2.8
	95.9

This summary shows that the most important sources of cash for the British Vita group in 1997 were the net cash inflow from operations and the net increase in loans. As already noted, the former should be clearly distinguished from the operating profit item in the consolidated profit and loss account. Operating profits are calculated not as cash is received or paid but as revenues or expenses are earned or incurred; that is, accrual accounting (see Chapter 4) is used, not cash accounting. Operating profits thus take account not just of increases and decreases in cash but also of depreciation and of changes in debtors, creditors and stocks. This is demonstrated in British Vita's note 24 [p. 42] which provides a reconciliation of the two concepts.

The most important uses of cash in 1997 were the purchase of new fixed assets, the payment of taxation, the payment of dividends, the purchase of subsidiary undertakings and the payment of interest. The tax and dividend figures are not the same as those in the group profit and loss account, but represent tax *paid* and dividends *paid*. The latter figure (£18.8 million) is easily checked [note 7, p. 30]. It is equal to the proposed ordinary dividends of 1996 (£9.4 million) (which were not paid until 1997) plus 1997's interim ordinary dividend of £9.4 million.

DEPRECIATION AND CASH FLOW

In the cash flow statement [p. 27] cash inflows and cash outflows refer to movements in cash. The term cash flow is sometimes used, perhaps more by financial analysts than accountants, to mean net profit plus depreciation. A more accurate term for cash flow in this sense would be working capital from operating activities, since, unlike cash flow from operating activities, no adjustment is made for increases/decreases in debtors, creditors and stocks.

It is important to understand that depreciation is neither a cash inflow nor a cash outflow. The cash outflow obviously took place when the fixed assets were originally bought. It would be double counting to regard each year's depreciation as a further cash outflow.

EVENTS AFTER THE BALANCE SHEET DATE

Important events may sometimes take place between the date of the balance sheet (e.g., 31 December 1997) and the date on which the balance sheet is approved by the board of directors for publication (e.g., 9 March 1998). An event which does not provide additional evidence of conditions existing at the balance sheet date (e.g., the acquisition of a new subsidiary in February 1998) is known as a 'non-adjusting event'. An example of an 'adjusting event', one which would require the financial statements to be altered if the amount was material, is the insolvency of a debtor as at the date of the balance sheet which only becomes known after that date but before the financial statements have been approved by the board.

CONTINGENCIES AND COMMITMENTS

Company law requires the disclosure in the notes of contingent liabilities and capital commitments. A contingency is a condition which exists at the balance sheet date, the outcome of which will be confirmed only on the occurrence or non-occurrence of one or more uncertain events. British Vita [p. 42, note 27] has a number of contingent liabilities; it has, for example, guaranteed some of the overdrafts and third-party liabilities of certain of its subsidiaries. It also has pension liabilities and contingent liabilities in respect of discounted bills of exchange.

As required by law, British Vita discloses in note 23 [p. 41] its commitments for capital expenditure not provided for in the accounts and capital expenditure authorized by the directors but not contracted for. The reader of the annual report thus has knowledge of important projected cash outlays in the forthcoming period. Also reported in this note are the group's annual commitments in respect of operating leases and details of finance lease arrangements entered into. Leasing and the difference between operating and finance leases is discussed in Chapter 8.

Taxation and Audit

> Taxation?
> Wherein? And what taxation? My Lord Cardinal,
> You that are blamed alike with us,
> Know you of this taxation?
> > William Shakespeare, *King Henry the Eighth*, I, ii

> Never ask of money spent
> Where the spender thinks it went
> Nobody was ever meant
> To remember or invent
> What he did with every cent
> > Robert Frost, 'The Hardship of Accounting'

This chapter deals briefly with two important matters of which all readers of company reports should have some knowledge: taxation and audit. No attempt will be made to go into either in detail; company taxation in particular can become fearsomely complicated. Furthermore, tax law is continually changing. In particular, the rules which applied to 'advance corporation tax' in 1997 have been abolished.

TAXATION IN THE ACCOUNTS

There are references to several forms of taxation in British Vita's 1997 annual report and accounts. Taxation relating to the profit on ordinary activities for the year ended 31 December 1997 is stated in the consolidated profit and loss account to be £22.2 million; that is, 34 per cent of the profit on ordinary activities before taxation of £66.2 million. In the group balance sheet, the current liabilities (creditors: amounts falling due within one year) include corporation tax of £17.6 million and other taxes and social security costs of £13.2 million [note 16, p. 36]. The provisions for liabilities and charges include deferred taxation of £4.4 million [note 19, p. 38]. The cash flow statement shows taxation paid of £15.6 million [p. 27]. Further details of the company's tax position are given in note 6 [p. 29]. Turnover is stated to exclude value added tax [p. 22].

CORPORATION TAX AND TAX CREDITS

British companies pay corporation tax, not income tax. Taxable income is measured in much the same way as accounting profit, but with many exceptions, the major one being depreciation. The corporation tax rate is usually set annually in arrears for the financial year 1 April to 31 March. The tax is *assessed*, however, on the basis of a company's accounting period. British Vita's accounting period ends, it will be remembered, on 31 December each year. The tax is payable for most companies nine months after the end of the financial year in which the company's accounting period ends. The rate of corporation tax can vary. In the financial year 1998 (i.e., from 1 April 1998 to 31 March 1999) it was 31 per cent. The lower rate of 21 per cent applied to companies with small profits. The basic rate of *income tax* (which is paid by shareholders) was 23 per cent.

Before 1 April 1999, when a dividend was paid by a company it also had to pay advance corporation tax (ACT), an advance payment on the corporation tax liability, to the Inland Revenue. Thereafter, corporation tax is payable in instalments, with payment dates not related to dividends. Shareholders are taxed on the dividend grossed up by a tax credit, but can set the tax credit against their liability to income tax. The example below, which assumes a corporation tax rate of 30 per cent and a starting rate of income tax of 10 per cent, shows how this 'imputation system', as it is called, works from the point of view of the shareholder.

Suppose, in the example, that the shareholder is a person (male), not a company, and holds 1 per cent of the shares. He would be assessed for income tax on £48,890, not £44,000. If he is a basic-rate taxpayer, he pays income tax at 10 per cent on these grossed-up dividends and therefore has no more tax to pay. If he is a higher-rate taxpayer, he has more tax to pay.

	£000
Taxable profit (assumed to be equal to accounting profit)	10,000
Corporation tax at 30%	3,000
Profit after tax	7,000
Dividend paid	4,400
Retained profit	2,600
The shareholders receive:	
dividend	4,400
plus tax credit (10/90 × £4,400,000)	489
	4,889

CAPITAL ALLOWANCES AND INVESTMENT INCENTIVES

As already noted in Chapter 2, capital allowances differ in amount from the depreciation shown in a company's accounts. The main reason for this is that whereas a company in reporting to its shareholders is interested in calculating profit as fairly as possible, the government may also be interested in trying to encourage investment.

The method of calculating capital allowances has varied from time to time, as have the rates allowed. At the time of writing, most capital allowances are given in the form of annual writing-down allowances calculated on the reducing balance method, as illustrated in the depreciation example in Chapter 2 (p. 21). The rates vary according to the class of asset. At the time of writing, the main rates are 25 per cent reducing balance on plant and machinery, and 4 per cent straight line on industrial buildings. There are no capital allowances on non-industrial buildings such as retail shops, offices and dwelling-houses.

It is important to note that all the allowances described above operate as deductions in the calculation of taxable income. If the latter is at least as large as the allowances, then the effect is to reduce the company's tax bill by the amount of the allowances multiplied by the corporation tax rate. A company which has no taxable income to offset against the allowances does not benefit at all.

This is not true of government grants. These are not reductions in taxable income but payments of cash to a company by the government. They are thus not dependent on the company making a taxable profit. The receipt of such grants does not affect capital allowances. It is standard accounting practice for grants relating to fixed assets to be credited to profit and loss account over the expected useful life of the asset, by treating the amount of the grant as a deferred credit (shown separately in the balance sheet), a portion of which is transferred to revenue annually. British Vita in 1997 credited government grants of £0.2 million to profit and loss account [note 3, p. 29]. Other grants are credited to revenue in the year in which the expenditure to which they relate is charged.

DEFERRED TAXATION

Capital allowances greater than accounting depreciation ('accelerated capital allowances') are an example of what is known as a 'timing difference'. The effect is to reduce taxable income in the current year below the company's profit before tax. It could be argued that the taxation payable has not been saved but merely 'deferred' to a later year. Whether, and if so how, a provision should be made for 'deferred taxation' is a matter which has aroused a lot of discussion in the accounting world. British Vita's policy in this matter is set out in its Accounting Policies [p. 23] as follows:

Deferred taxation is provided using the liability method in respect of timing differences except where the liability is not expected to arise in the foreseeable future. Advance corporation tax which is available to reduce the corporation tax payable on future profits is carried forward where recovery is reasonably assured and, to the extent appropriate, is deducted from the provision for deferred taxation.

British Vita thus, in accordance with standard accounting practice, makes provision not for all potential future deferred tax payable but only for that part where there is a reasonable probability that payment will have to be made in the foreseeable future (usually regarded as the next three years). Note 19 [p. 38] discloses that 'full' provision for deferred tax would have amounted to £6 million, as distinct from the 'partial' provision made of £4.4 million.

CAPITAL GAINS TAX

Individuals are taxed not only on their income but also on certain capital gains; that is, the excess of the price they receive on selling an asset over the price they paid for it. They are entitled to an annual exempt amount on which the tax is not payable. Companies are not liable to capital gains tax on their capital gains, which are instead charged to corporation tax.

Tax does not become payable when an asset is revalued unless it is sold and even then the tax is postponed if a replacement is bought. Since fixed assets are held for use rather than sale and would generally be replaced if sold, it is not the practice to make provision for the tax which would arise if the assets were sold for the revalued amount [note 19, p. 38].

CLOSE COMPANIES

The Finance Act 1965 introduced the concept of the 'close company', defined as a company resident in the United Kingdom which is under the control of five or fewer participators and associates or of participants who are directors. The detailed legislation is extremely complex but has been of little practical importance since 1980. British Vita states in the Directors' Report that it is not a close company [p. 18].

VALUE ADDED TAX

Unlike the forms of taxation discussed so far, value added tax (VAT) is not a direct tax but an indirect tax; that is, one which is not assessed and collected from those intended to bear it (the final consumers). VAT is a multi-stage tax; manufacturing companies such as British Vita pay tax on their inputs, charge tax on their outputs and can set off the tax paid against the tax charged. Sales and purchases are included in the consolidated profit and loss account net of VAT, but trade debtors and trade creditors in the balance sheet include VAT.

TAX LAW

The most important statutes (Acts of Parliament) relating to the taxes described in this chapter are the Income and Corporation Taxes Act 1988, the Capital Allowances Act 1990, the Taxation of Chargeable Gains Act 1992 and the Taxes Management Act 1970. Every year there is at least one Finance Act amending the law. There is also a large body of case law relating to taxation.

AUDIT REPORTS

As mentioned in the Directors' Responsibility Statement [p. 45], the preparation of the financial statements of a company and their presentation to the shareholders are the duties of the directors, not of the auditors, although the latter may give valuable assistance.

The Report of the Auditors to the shareholders of British Vita PLC [p. 46] reads as follows:

Auditors' report to the Shareholders of British Vita PLC
We have audited the accounts on pages 24 to 44 which have been prepared under the historical cost convention, as modified by the revaluation of certain fixed assets, and the accounting policies set out on pages 22 and 23.

Respective responsibilities of directors and auditors

As described on page 45 the Company's directors are responsible for the preparation of the accounts and it is our responsibility to form an independent opinion, based on our audit, on those accounts and to report our opinion to you.

Basis of opinion

We conducted our audit in accordance with Auditing Standards issued by the Auditing Practices Board. An audit includes examination, on a test basis, of evidence relevant to the amounts and disclosures in the accounts. It also includes an assessment of the significant estimates and judgements made by the directors in the preparation of the accounts and of whether the accounting policies are appropriate to the circumstances of the Company and of the Group, consistently applied and adequately disclosed.

We planned and performed our audit so as to obtain all the information and explanations which we considered necessary in order to provide us with sufficient evidence to give reasonable assurance that the accounts are free from material misstatement, whether caused by fraud or other irregularity or error. In forming our opinion we also evaluated the overall adequacy of the presentation of information in the accounts.

Opinion

In our opinion the accounts give a true and fair view of the state of affairs of the Company and of the Group at 31 December 1997 and of the Group's profit and cash flows for the year then ended and have been properly prepared in accordance with the Companies Act 1985.

The report is signed by Arthur Andersen and dated 9 March 1998, the same date on which the accounts were approved by the board of directors [p. 26]. Arthur Andersen are one of the 'Big Five' international accounting firms; the audits of UK listed companies are increasingly carried out by members of these firms. Arthur Andersen sign as 'Chartered Accountants and Registered Auditors'. This dual description recognizes firstly that the firm's partners are members of a British professional accountancy body and secondly that the firm's name is inscribed on a statutory register as qualified for appointment as a company auditor. All three Institutes of Chartered Accountants (in England and Wales, of Scotland, in Ireland) provide, as does also the Association of Chartered Certified Accountants, a recognized professional qualification for company auditors, and keep registers.

There are a number of interesting points to note about the auditors' report:

1. It is a report, not a certificate or guarantee: the auditors report their opinion; they do not certify or guarantee anything.
2. What they give their opinion on is compliance with the Companies Act and the 'truth and fairness' of the accounts. This is not the same as saying that the accounts are 'correct' or 'right' in every particular. It should be clear from the discussion of the financial statements in Chapter 2 that figures in balance sheets, profit and loss accounts and cash flow statements are necessarily based to a certain extent on estimates and judgements made by the directors, and on a particular set of rules.
3. Reference is made to the basis on which the financial statements have been prepared. In the UK this is normally the historical cost convention, often modified by the revaluation of fixed assets. As will be seen in Chapter 4, a few UK companies follow the current cost convention.
4. The auditors are reporting to the shareholders of British Vita, not to the directors. Their function, as a late-nineteenth-century English judge put it, is to serve as a 'watchdog' for the shareholders. They are appointed by the shareholders, usually on the recommendation of the directors. Appointment is made each year by resolution at the annual general meeting.
5. The auditors do not report on whether or not frauds have been committed but limit themselves to stating that they have sought reasonable assurance that the financial statements are free of material misstatements caused by fraud.
6. A careful distinction is made between the respective responsibilities of the directors and the auditors.
7. A brief description is given of the way in which an audit is carried out, with a reference to the auditing standards issued by the Auditing Practices Board (APB).

The report set out above is suitable when the auditors give an unqualified opinion. Occasionally auditors give a qualified opinion or are even unable to form an opinion (known as 'disclaimer of opinion'). Qualified opinions may arise if there is a limitation on the scope of the auditors' examination

or the auditors are in disagreement with the directors on the treatment
or disclosure of a matter in the financial statements.

AUDIT EXPECTATIONS GAP

The wording of UK audit reports is an amalgam of legal requirements
and of what the accountancy profession considers to be the function of
the audit. This does not necessarily coincide with what all users of audit
reports would prefer and in recent years there has been a recognition of
what is known as the 'audit expectations gap'.

A discussion document, *Auditing into the Twenty-first Century*, issued
by the Research Committee of the Institute of Chartered Accountants of
Scotland in 1993 identified these public expectations as follows:

(1) the financial statements are right;
(2) the company will not fail;
(3) there has been no fraud;
(4) the company has acted within the law;
(5) the company has been competently managed;
(6) the company has adopted a responsible attitude to environmental
and societal matters;
(7) the external auditors are independent of the directors;
(8) the external auditors will report to a third party if they suspect
that the directors are involved in fraud or other illegal activity;
(9) the external auditors are accountable to a wide range of stakeholders;
(10) the external auditors are financially liable if they fail in any of
their duties.

Some of these expectations are already being met in full or in part, but
neither the government nor the accountancy profession is likely to accept
that all of them are reasonable, in the sense that there is an effective
demand for them and there are auditors capable of supplying them at a
reasonable cost.

We have already seen that no financial statements can be regarded as
'right' as distinct from 'true and fair'. Auditors are likely to continue to

report on the latter. Neither the directors nor its auditors can guarantee that a company will not fail but directors can reasonably be expected to state, and auditors to report on, whether or not a company is likely to remain a going concern for the ensuing twelve months. Auditors cannot guarantee that there has been no material fraud but they can report whether or not there are systems of internal control which minimize opportunities for fraud and maximize the likelihood that any such fraud will be quickly detected. Similarly, while auditors cannot guarantee that a company has in all respects acted within the law, they can confirm that there are internal control systems which minimize the opportunities for committing illegal acts and maximize the likelihood of speedy detection.

On the other hand, auditors, as experts in accounting and finance, are not necessarily qualified to assess the competence of management or to report on environmental and societal matters, although these could well be the subject of a separate 'environmental audit' for those few companies (e.g., British Polythene) which publish an 'environmental report'.

It is obviously important that auditors should not only be skilled in their profession but also be, and be seen to be, independent of the directors and managers of the company being audited. Company law requires that an auditor must not be an officer or servant of the company or of any company in the group, or a partner or employee of such officer or servant. The amount of the auditors' remuneration must be stated in the annual report. For the British Vita group in 1997 it was £0.7 million [note 3, p. 29]. Auditors may (and commonly do) also provide other services (e.g., taxation advice) to companies, although some commentators argue that this may endanger their independence. The amount received for any such services must be separately disclosed. For the British Vita group in 1997 it was £0.2 million [note 3, p. 29]. Like many listed companies British Vita has established an audit committee composed of non-executives. Its function is to review the half year and annual financial statements and matters related to both external audit and internal audit [p. 16].

Auditors of financial institutions are already required to report to a regulatory body when they are satisfied that it is necessary to do so in order to protect the interests of shareholders or depositors. It is possible that, despite the problems of confidentiality, this obligation may be extended to other types of companies.

As already noted, the external auditors are accountable to, and report to, the shareholders, although their report is also in practice relied upon by other stakeholders in the company. It can be argued, therefore, that auditors ought to be legally liable to other stakeholders as well. The House of Lords upheld, however, in the Caparo case (1990) that auditors owe a duty of care to the shareholders as a whole, not to individual shareholders or to other persons. This decision has been much criticized.

Accounting Regulation and Accounting Concepts

REGULATION

In order to draw up a set of financial statements for a company it is necessary to make decisions about:

(1) what should be disclosed (*disclosure*);
(2) the format of the statements (*presentation*);
(3) the rules of recognition, measurement and valuation (*measurement*).

Who should make these decisions; that is, how, if at all, should company financial statements be regulated? There are a number of possibilities:

(1) Each company is allowed to decide for itself.
(2) A private-sector body composed wholly, mainly or partly of accountants, as acknowledged experts in the field, makes the decisions.
(3) The state makes the decisions by means of, for example,
    (i) legislation;
    (ii) a government-appointed regulatory body;
    (iii) a national accounting plan;
    (iv) an accounting court.

It is possible, of course, that a mixture of the above methods may be appropriate.

Whichever methods are chosen, there are costs and benefits. No one method is likely to be ideal for all countries and at all times. In this chapter we shall look at the British approach in the late 1990s. It has to be remembered that it is the result of a century and a half of evolution and that British ideas on the subject are strongly influenced by the United States and by other member states of the European Union.

During the nineteenth century most British companies were allowed complete freedom in matters of disclosure, presentation and measurement. During the first half of the twentieth century it gradually became accepted that, while the government should not interfere with presentation and measurement, it ought to prescribe by legislation what should be disclosed. This was the general philosophy behind the Companies Act 1948. The Act imposed two obligations on company directors: firstly, to prepare balance sheets and profit and loss accounts which gave a 'true and fair view' and, secondly, to give the detailed information specified in a Schedule to the Act. No definition was given of the phrase 'true and fair'.

This approach was commented on favourably in the report of the 1962 committee on company law amendment:

In our view the general scheme of the Act in this respect is the right one, namely to indicate in general terms the objectives and the standard of disclosure required and also to prescribe certain specific information that must be given. The formula 'true and fair' seems to us satisfactory as an indication of the required standard, while it makes for certainty to prescribe certain specific information which the law regards as the minimum necessary for the purpose of attaining that standard.

(*Report of the Company Law Committee*, Cmnd 1749, HMSO, 1962, para. 332)

The committee went on to state that 'it is primarily to the initiative of the professional associations that we must look if the general principles of the Act are to be effectively applied in practice' (para. 334). They referred in particular to the Recommendations on Accounting Principles issued periodically by the Institute of Chartered Accountants in England and Wales. It was through these Recommendations (issued between 1942 and 1969) that the professional accountancy bodies began to involve themselves in matters of disclosure and measurement.

During the 1960s the quality of published financial statements was increasingly criticized. The profession, encouraged by the government, responded in 1970 with the establishment of an Accounting Standards

Committee (ASC). The ASC was replaced in 1990 by the Accounting Standards Board (ASB) (see below).

The British government has made no serious attempt to control company financial statements through a regulatory agency (as exists in the United States in the form of the Securities and Exchange Commission) or a national accounting plan (as in France). It has, however, intervened on matters of disclosure and in the debate about inflation accounting (see below) and, as a result of Britain's entry into the European Union, has legislated on presentation and measurement.

In Britain, then, it is company legislation and accounting standards which largely determine what goes into published financial statements. Less important influences are tax legislation and the requirements of the Stock Exchange. Tax legislation influences published accounts because companies (especially small companies) may find it inconvenient to follow one set of practices for tax purposes and another for reporting to shareholders. Accounting practices banned for tax calculations tend to be unpopular in published financial statements, but there is no compulsion for a company to follow tax rules in those statements. Indeed, several tax treatments are not followed in financial reporting. A good example is the difference between depreciation and capital allowances (see Chapter 3). In this respect Britain differs from most Continental European countries. Stock Exchange requirements for listed companies do not go much beyond those of company law and accounting standards.

The detailed requirements of the Companies Act 1985, as amended in 1989, are summarized in the Glossary (Appendix B) under a number of headings, the most important of which are: Debtors, Directors' Emoluments, Directors' Report, Distributable Reserves, Employee Information, Liabilities, Segmental Reporting, True and Fair View, Turnover and Undistributable Reserves.

FORMATS

Companies have a choice of two balance sheet formats and four profit and loss account formats. The minimum requirements of one of the balance sheet formats are illustrated in Table 4.1. The other format is very similar except that it is set out horizontally rather than vertically.

Headings for which there is no balance may be omitted, and additional detail may be added. British Vita, for example, has omitted the heading 'Intangible assets'.

The four profit and loss account formats are more flexible. Two are vertical and two horizontal. Most companies publish a profit and loss account very much like British Vita's, but others disclose the costs of raw materials and consumables, staff costs and depreciation, instead of costs of sales, distribution costs and administrative expenses.

Table 4.1. Balance Sheet Format

Fixed assets			
Intangible assets	×		
Tangible assets	×		
Investments	×		
			×
Current assets			
Stocks	×		
Debtors	×		
Investments	×		
Cash at bank and in hand	×		
		×	
Creditors: amounts falling due within one year		(×)	
Net current assets (liabilities)			×
Total assets less current liabilities			× ×
Creditors: amounts falling due after more than one year			×
Provisions for liabilities and charges			×
Capital and reserves			
Called up share capital	×		
Share premium account	×		
Revaluation reserve	×		
Other reserves	×		
Profit and loss account	×		×
			×
Minority interests			×
			× ×

The directors of small companies (defined in terms of total assets, turnover and average number of employees) have the privilege of preparing and filing abbreviated accounts with the Registrar of Companies if they so wish and may also send shorter-form (but not abbreviated) financial statements to their shareholders. Medium-sized companies are granted some exemptions in what they can file with the Registrar of Companies, but must send a full set of financial statements to shareholders. Subsidiaries may use the abbreviations only if the group to which they belong is as a whole small or medium. No public companies may be regarded as small or medium. Small and medium *groups* are exempted from filing consolidated accounts with the Registrar.

SUMMARY FINANCIAL STATEMENTS

The cost of sending out a full set of financial statements to all shareholders is quite considerable, especially for companies such as BG, which, as noted in Chapter 1, has over 1.25 million shareholders. It is probably for this reason that listed companies are permitted to issue financial statements which summarize the information contained in the annual accounts and directors' report. The issue of summary financial statements is optional (British Vita, with far fewer shareholders than BG, does not issue them) and shareholders who state that they wish to receive the full accounts must be sent them. The form of summary financial statements is prescribed by regulation and comprises the main items from the directors' report, consolidated profit and loss account, and balance sheet. Summary financial statements are not necessarily simpler to understand than a full set of statements.

ACCOUNTING STANDARDS

The Accounting Standards Board (ASB) is prescribed under company law as an accounting standards setting body. The Companies Act requires companies (other than small and medium companies) to state whether their accounts have been prepared in accordance with 'applicable accounting standards' and to give particulars of any material departure from those standards and the reasons for them. The ASB issues Financial Reporting Standards (FRSs) and has also adopted the extant Statements of Standard Accounting Practice (SSAPs) issued by the Accounting Standards Committee (ASC). SSAPs are gradually being replaced by FRSs. Small companies need comply with only one standard: the Financial Reporting Standard for Smaller Entities (FRSSE).

The ASB has ten members appointed by the Financial Reporting Council. The chairman and the technical director are full time, the other members part time. (The ASC had more than twice as many members but all were part time.) The members of the ASB are drawn from the accountancy profession, commerce, industry, the City of London, the public sector and academe. Unlike the former ASC, the ASB is independent of the member bodies of the Consultative Committee of Accountancy Bodies (the Institute of Chartered Accountants in England and Wales, the Institute of Chartered Accountants of Scotland, the Institute of Chartered Accountants in Ireland, the Association of Chartered Certified Accountants, the Chartered Institute of Management Accountants and the Chartered Institute of Public Finance and Accountancy) and issues accounting standards on its own authority. However, it only issues an FRS after extensive consultation, which always includes an 'exposure draft' for comment by interested parties.

As at 31 May 1999, fifteen FRSs had been issued and thirteen SSAPs were still extant for large entities:

FRSs
1. Cash flow statements
2. Accounting for subsidiary undertakings
3. Reporting financial performance
4. Capital instruments
5. Reporting the substance of transactions
6. Acquisitions and mergers
7. Fair values in acquisition accounting
8. Related party disclosures
9. Associates and joint ventures
10. Goodwill and intangible assets

11. Impairment of fixed assets and goodwill
12. Provisions, contingent liabilities and contingent assets
13. Derivatives and other financial instruments: disclosures
14. Earnings per share
15. Tangible fixed assets

SSAPs
2. Disclosure of accounting policies
4. Accounting for government grants
5. Accounting for value added tax
8. The treatment of taxation under the imputation system in the accounts of companies
9. Stocks and long-term contracts
13. Accounting for research and development
15. Accounting for deferred tax
17. Accounting for post balance sheet events
19. Accounting for investment properties
20. Foreign currency translation
21. Accounting for leases and hire purchase contracts
24. Accounting for pension costs
25. Segmental reporting

The ASC also approved the issue of non-mandatory Statements of Recommended Practice (SORPs). It prepared and issued SORPs on pension scheme accounts and accounting by charities. SORPs have also been issued by other bodies, such as the Oil Industry Accounting Committee, and approved by the ASC. The ASB does not issue or approve ('frank') SORPs. An Urgent Issues Task Force (UITF) assists the ASB in areas where an accounting standard or legal requirement exists, but where unsatisfactory or conflicting interpretations have developed or appear likely to develop. The UITF seeks to reach a consensus to which companies are expected to conform.

One reason for the replacement of the ASC by the ASB was the difficulty that the former had in persuading companies to comply with accounting standards issued by professional accountancy bodies with no legal right to lay down measurement rules or to say what must be disclosed in company financial statements. The ASB's standards, unlike those of the ASC, have the recognition of law. In addition, a Financial Reporting

Review Panel was set up in 1991 under the Companies Act. The main task of the panel is to examine material departures from company law and accounting standards by companies. The panel is empowered to apply to the court for a declaration that the accounts of a company do not comply with the requirements of the Act and for an order requiring the company's directors to prepare revised accounts. In practice, companies have so far always agreed to rectify their accounts without the intervention of the court and the panel is an important means of ensuring compliance with accounting standards.

FRSs and SSAPs are very important and references to them will be found throughout this book. The ways in which accounting standards are set or should be set have been much discussed. To some extent standard setting is inevitably a 'political' process since standard setting bodies, to be effective, must take account of the sometimes conflicting interests of the users and preparers of financial statements. Standard setters often prefer, however, to take account as far as possible of a conceptual framework, a set of interrelated concepts underlying the procedures of financial accounting. Adherence to such a framework helps to ensure that accounting standards have some internal consistency. Explicit conceptual frameworks have been drawn up in the United States and Australia and also by the International Accounting Standards Committee (of which the UK professional accountancy bodies are members). The ASB has issued drafts of its *Statement of Principles for Financial Reporting*.

The most general accounting standard is SSAP 2 on the disclosure of accounting policies. This sets out four basic assumptions or concepts which are said to underlie the periodic accounts of business enterprises:

1. The 'going concern' concept: the enterprise will continue in operational existence for the foreseeable future.
2. The 'accruals' concept: revenue and costs are accrued (that is, recognized as they are earned or incurred, not as money is received or paid), matched with one another as far as their relationship can be established or justifiably assumed, and dealt with in the profit and loss account of the period to which they relate.
3. The 'consistency' concept: there is consistency of accounting treatment of like items within each accounting period and from one period to the next.

4. The 'prudence' concept: revenue and profits are not anticipated, but are recognized by inclusion in the profit and loss account only when realized in the form either of cash or of other assets the ultimate realization of which can be assessed with reasonable certainty; provision is made for all known liabilities whether the amount of these is known with certainty or is a best estimate in the light of the information available.

As a result of SSAP 2, companies publish statements of 'accounting policies' setting out the way in which they have dealt with a number of matters. British Vita's statement, for example [pp. 22–3], covers the basis of the accounts (i.e., the historical cost convention modified to include the revaluation of certain fixed assets), the basis of consolidation, foreign currency, stocks, turnover, leases, depreciation of tangible fixed assets, grants, research and development, patents and trade marks, pension costs and deferred taxation.

CONCEPTUAL FRAMEWORK

The ASB's Statement deals with accounting concepts in great detail, covering the objective of financial statements, the qualitative characteristics of financial information, the elements of financial statements, recognition in financial statements, measurement in financial statements, presentation of financial information, and the reporting entity. The emphasis of the Statement is on meeting the information needs of users of financial statements, and more particularly investors in companies, who need to assess the stewardship of the management and to make decisions about buying, selling and holding shares. Qualitative characteristics are those that make financial information useful. Ideally, such information should be relevant (have either predictive or confirmatory value) and reliable (provide a faithful representation, emphasize substance rather than form, be free from bias, be prudent and be complete). It should also be comparable and understandable. In practice there may have to be a trade-off between these characteristics. For example, completely reliable information may not be sufficiently timely to be relevant to action by users.

The elements of financial statements are, as discussed in Chapter 2, assets, liabilities, ownership interest (shareholders' funds, in the case of a company), gains and losses, contributions from owners and distributions to owners. The ASB's Statement provides definitions of all of these. The existence of an asset or a liability does not necessarily mean that it should be 'recognized' in a financial statement; that is, depicted in both words and monetary amount and included in a statement total. Assets and liabilities are recognized only if there is sufficient evidence that a change has occurred and that it can be measured as a monetary amount with sufficient reliability. Recognition is usually triggered by transactions but other events (e.g., damage caused by a fire) may also act as a trigger. Such events may, however, be difficult to measure.

The Statement discusses two broad measurement systems: historical cost and current value. In practice, as noted in Chapter 2, most UK companies follow historical cost but modify it by carrying some fixed assets at a valuation, although not necessarily a completely current one. In times of inflation, prices in general may change considerably over time. Table 4.2 shows the fall in the domestic purchasing power of the 'pound in the pocket'. Prices increased fourfold between 1976 and 1997. Current value can be defined as the lower of an asset's replacement cost and recoverable amount. An asset's recoverable amount is its value in its most profitable use; that is, the higher of its value in use (the net present value of future cash flows obtainable as a result of its continued use) and its net realizable value. A reduction in the recoverable value of a fixed asset (including goodwill) must be recognized in the financial statements as an 'impairment loss'.

The Companies Act distinguishes between 'historical cost accounting rules' which require the application to financial statements of conventional accounting procedures based on historical cost modified by prudence, and 'alternative accounting rules' which permit not only the use of current cost valuations but also a mixture of historical and current valuations. British Vita, like many other companies, prepares its financial statements 'under the historical cost convention modified to include the revaluation of certain fixed assets' [p. 22].

In times of inflation, such as those experienced in the 1970s, balance sheet values based on historical cost rapidly become divorced from current values, and profits may be overstated. This is most easily understood in relation to fixed assets and depreciation. If fixed assets are valued at

Table 4.2. Inflation Rates, 1974–98

	Index (average for calendar year)	Percentage increase over the previous year
1974	27.5	—
1975	34.2	24.4
1976	39.8	16.4
1977	46.1	15.8
1978	50.0	8.5
1979	56.7	13.4
1980	66.8	17.8
1981	74.8	12.0
1982	81.2	8.6
1983	84.9	4.6
1984	89.2	5.1
1985	94.6	6.1
1986	97.8	3.4
1987	101.9	4.2
1988	106.9	4.9
1989	115.1	7.8
1990	126.1	9.2
1991	133.5	5.9
1992	138.5	3.7
1993	140.7	1.6
1994	144.1	2.4
1995	149.1	3.5
1996	152.7	2.4
1997	157.5	3.1
1998		3.4

Source. Index of Retail Prices (1 January 1987 = 100) as reported in *Accountancy*.

historical cost, depreciation will usually be based on historical cost as well. This will result in a lower depreciation charge, and hence a higher profit, than if both the asset and the depreciation were written up to, say, current replacement cost. It can reasonably be argued that the use of historical costs during a period of inflation can lead to the publication of profit figures which are in part fictitious. The distribution of such profits would mean a running down of the *real* (as opposed to the money) capital of the company.

However, the attempts by the ASC to introduce some form of accounting for inflation were beset by many difficulties. Two principal methods of accounting for inflation were debated:

1. Adjustments of changes in the *general* price level only; that is, current purchasing power (CPP) accounting.
2. Adjustments for changes in *specific* prices; that is, current cost accounting (CCA).

The ASC originally preferred CPP accounting, and this was the basis of the provisional SSAP 7 issued in 1974. The government-appointed Sandilands Committee, however, which reported in 1975, rejected CPP accounting in favour of CCA. The standard finally accepted in 1980, SSAP 16, was CCA based. However, lower rates of inflation and controversy about the details of the standard made SSAP 16 difficult to enforce, and it is no longer mandatory. Like most companies, British Vita provides no CCA data in its 1997 annual report. Only a few listed UK companies, most of them public utilities, provide such data. One example is BG plc.

The ASB believes that practice should develop by evolving in the direction of the greater use of current values to the extent that this is consistent with the constraints of reliability and cost.

ACCOUNTING FOR FOREIGN EXCHANGE

British Vita's subsidiaries and associated undertakings outside the UK normally keep their accounts in the appropriate local currency. Table 4.3 shows the fluctuations of the pound sterling in relation to the US dollar, the world's major currency. These foreign financial statements are translated using year-end rates of exchange; that is, by the 'closing rate' method. This is the method that standard accounting practice requires for subsidiaries which operate as separate or quasi-independent entities. Companies can choose under this method to translate *profit and loss account* items at either closing rates or average rates for the year. The latter is gaining in popularity. British Vita changed to average rates in 1993.

A high percentage of British Vita's sales are made outside the UK, especially in Continental Europe, so the increasing strength of the pound sterling in 1997 [note 2, p. 28] reduced the translated sterling value of its turnover. In his review [p. 3] the chief executive states that turnover from continuing operations increased 4 per cent in volume during 1997 but, mainly because of the adverse translation effects, decreased by 7 per cent in value (from £873.5 million to £808.4 million). The translation effect would have been even more adverse if closing rates had been used.

If the rates at the end of the period differ from those obtaining at the beginning of the year, an exchange or translation difference will arise. Under the closing rate method such gains or losses are dealt with through reserves and do not affect the profit for the financial year. In a world of sharply fluctuating exchange rates, exchange differences can be quite large. British Vita in 1997 recorded negative exchange rate differences of £12.8 million [note 21, p. 41] equal to 29 per cent of its profit for the financial year of £43.8 million.

Table 4.3. The Rate of Exchange of £1 to US$1, 1974–98

31 December	1974	2.35
	1975	2.02
	1976	1.70
	1977	1.91
	1978	2.03
	1979	2.22
	1980	2.38
	1981	1.91
	1982	1.62
	1983	1.45
	1984	1.16
	1985	1.45
	1986	1.47
	1987	1.87
	1988	1.81
	1989	1.61
	1990	1.93
	1991	1.87
	1992	1.51
	1993	1.48
	1994	1.56
	1995	1.55
	1996	1.70
	1997	1.65
	1998	1.66

Source. UN Monthly Bulletin of Statistics.

An alternative method of foreign currency translation is the so-called 'temporal method', which is used where the operations of the foreign entity are regarded as an integral part of those of the parent company. The temporal method differs from the closing rate method in that those assets recorded in the local currency accounts at historical cost rather than at a current value (that is, fixed assets and most stocks) are translated at the rates ruling at the dates of acquisition. Also, and very importantly, exchange gains and losses are passed through the profit and loss account. Under the temporal method, groups whose parent company's currency is strengthening tend to show translation gains, while those whose parent company's currency is weakening tend to show translation losses. This method is found much more in the US than in the UK.

For foreign entities whose economies are experiencing very high rates of inflation ('hyper-inflation'), British standard accounting practice requires before application of the closing rate method either restatement of the financial statements to take account of local inflation or for the subsidiary to keep its accounts in an appropriate non-local currency (e.g., US dollars).

Foreign exchange *transactions* are translated into sterling at the appropriate forward contract rate or rate of exchange at the date of the transactions.

CREATIVE ACCOUNTING

Financial statements can be used to mislead users as well as to inform them. Such 'creative accounting' became more common in the UK from the 1980s, intensifying the conflict between legal form and economic substance. Creative accounting usually involves emphasizing the letter of accounting rules rather than their spirit. The overriding requirement to give a true and fair view should be able to prevent this but it has not always succeeded in doing so in practice, so the ASB has had to combat it in FRSs. Much ingenuity has been devoted to maximizing earnings per share, improving liquidity by window-dressing and minimizing gearing ratios. There is discussion of each of these in Chapters 7 and 8.

5 Tools of Analysis and Sources of Information

> ... high Heaven rejects the lore
> Of nicely-calculated less or more.
> > William Wordsworth, 'Inside of King's College Chapel,
> > Cambridge'

The first four chapters of this book have been mainly descriptive. In the chapters which follow we turn to analysis and interpretation. We shall be concerned with three main questions:

1. Is the company under analysis making a satisfactory profit?
2. Is the company likely to run out of cash, or to keep cash idle?
3. How does the company decide the sources of its long-term funds?

These are the related problems of profitability, liquidity and capital structure.

Our tools of analysis will be the relationships which exist among the different items in the financial statements ('financial ratios') and the rates of return linking outflows with expected inflows ('yields').

FINANCIAL RATIOS

Financial ratios are normally expressed either as percentages or by the number of times one figure can be divided into another. For example, if a company has current assets of £10,000 and current liabilities of £5,000, we could say that current liabilities are 50 per cent of current assets, that current assets are 200 per cent of current liabilities, that the ratio $\dfrac{\text{current assets}}{\text{current liabilities}}$ is 2.0 or that the ratio $\dfrac{\text{current liabilities}}{\text{current assets}}$ is 0.5. Which method is chosen is a matter of convenience and convention. In the example quoted it is customary to speak of a current ratio, $\dfrac{\text{current assets}}{\text{current liabilities}}$, of 2.0. (A percentage, as can be seen from the above, is merely a ratio multiplied by 100.)

Not all ratios and percentages are significant or useful, and one must guard against the temptation to calculate them for their own sake. The component parts of a ratio must be reasonably related to each other and measure something important. It is unlikely, for example, that much can be gained from a scrutiny of the relationship between current liabilities and goodwill. The limitations of conventional historical cost accounting must always be kept in mind, and accounting figures should not be treated as more precise than they really are. There is little sense in calculating a ratio to more than two decimal places.

A single ratio in isolation seldom provides much information. Each ratio calculated should either provide additional confirmation of what has already been deduced or act as a guide to the further questions which need to be asked.

YIELDS

A yield is a rate of return relating outflows to inflows. If, for example, I buy for £50 an irredeemable government bond with a par value of £100 on which interest of 4 per cent is payable annually, there is an immediate cash outflow of £50, followed by a series of cash inflows of £4 each year in perpetuity. The yield (gross of tax) is $\dfrac{4 \times 100}{50}$ per cent (i.e., 8 per cent). If the bond were redeemable at a fixed price at some date in the future, there would be a difference between the flat yield, which takes only the interest into account, and the redemption yield, which takes the redemption price into account as well. For example, if the bond is redeemable twenty years hence at par, the flat yield is about 5.0 per cent and the redemption yield about 9.8 per cent.

THE NEED FOR COMPARISONS

As already noted, any ratio, percentage or yield is of little value in isolation. It is necessary to have some standard with which to compare it. The standard can be a budgeted one, set by the company for itself; a historical one, based on the past performance of the company; or an industry one, based on the observed ratios of companies in the same industry.

Budgeted standards are not usually available to shareholders or external financial analysts. Historical comparisons are often given in annual reports: see, for example, p. 6 of British Vita's report, headed 'Summary of Financial Data 1993–1997'. This presents information in the form both of raw data (e.g., turnover, operating profit) and ratios (e.g., operating profit as a percentage of turnover).

INDUSTRY RATIOS

Industry ratios pose a much more difficult problem to the financial analyst. There are a number of reasons for this.

Firstly, it is often difficult to decide to which industry a company belongs. Many industries are, in fact, composed of a surprisingly hetero-geneous group of companies. In the Stock Exchange industrial classi-fication at the date on which its 1997 annual report was published, British Vita is included in the 'chemicals, advanced materials' group, which includes only five other companies (the Scapa Group,which is about the same size as British Vita, and four much smaller companies). The broader 'chemicals' group comprises 39 companies, some of which (e.g., ICI and the BOC Group) are very much larger than British Vita. (The standard industrial classification used in government publications is not identical with the Stock Exchange classification and both are revised from time to time. In this book we shall follow the custom of most financial analysts in using the latter.)

Secondly, the emphasis of the system of accounting at present in use is more on *consistency* for a particular company over time, than on *comparability* among different companies at a single point in time, and analysts must constantly be on their guard against differences in definition and in methods of measurement.

Thirdly, companies end their accounting periods on different dates, so that industry ratios are perforce averages of ratios calculated at different dates and for different periods.

For these reasons not too much reliance can be placed on an industry comparison which is based on ratios obtained from published accounts. Individual and industry ratios are, however, available on a commercial basis from a number of sources, including Dun & Bradstreet, Extel and Datastream.

SOURCES OF INFORMATION

In this section are listed a number of useful sources of information relating to individual companies, to industries or to the company sector as a whole. The list is not intended to be exhaustive. Most of the items should be available in a good public or university library.

1. *Sources of UK Business Information* by Desmond Crone, Catherine Gillett and Louise Tippett (1995, no. 331 in the Accountants Digest series published by Accountancy Books, Institute of Chartered Accountants in England and Wales).
2. *The Times 1000* (published annually by Times Books). This lists each year, among other things, the thousand largest UK companies (ranked by capital employed), with details of their capital employed (defined as shareholders' funds plus long-term loans plus intra-group payables plus deferred liabilities); turnover; pre-tax profit; number of employees; and the market capitalization of the equity (i.e., the total market value of all the company's ordinary shares). British Vita is in the top 300 of the thousand.
3. *Financial Statistics* (published monthly by the Government Statistical Service; an 'explanatory handbook' is published annually). Section 8 provides data about companies.

4. *British Business* (published weekly by the Department of Trade and Industry).
5. *Economic Trends* (published monthly by the Government Statistical Service).
6. *Bank of England Quarterly Bulletin*.
7. *United Kingdom National Accounts* (the 'Blue Book'; published annually by the Government Statistical Service).
8. *Stock Exchange Yearbook* (published annually by Macmillan for the London Stock Exchange). This provides a wealth of information on all aspects of the UK stock market. The Exchange also publishes monthly Fact Sheets.
9. *Financial Reporting Today: Current and Emerging Issues* (published annually by Accountancy Books, Institute of Chartered Accountants in England and Wales).
10. *Accounting Standards* (published annually by the Institute of Chartered Accountants in England and Wales). This contains the full texts of all UK exposure drafts and accounting standards extant at 1 May each year. It also contains background material on the Accounting Standards Board.
11. *Companies Accounts Checklists* by S. G. Hastie (1997, no. 383 in the Accountants Digest series; revised and updated periodically).

6 Profitability, Return on Investment and Value Added

For what is Worth in anything
But so much Money as 'twill bring.

Samuel Butler, *Hudibras*, I, i

PROFITABILITY

One of the first questions a shareholder is likely to ask of a company is whether it is making a profit. If so, is it making a satisfactory profit? We have already encountered some of the difficulties which arise in trying to measure profit. Although accountants try to make measurements as objective as possible, many financial numbers, even those purporting to represent past events, are necessarily to some extent estimates. Profit calculations are especially affected by the difficulties of measuring depreciation and valuing stock-in-trade, difficulties which are accentuated in times of changing price levels and fluctuating exchange rates.

RETURN ON INVESTMENT

Sales (turnover) and profits should not be looked at in isolation from the investment in net assets made to achieve them. The relationship between them can be set out as follows:

$$\text{Return on investment (ROI)} = \frac{\text{profit}}{\text{net assets}} = \frac{\text{profit}}{\text{sales}} \times \frac{\text{sales}}{\text{net assets}}$$

As already noted, there are a number of 'profit' figures in British Vita's consolidated profit and loss account; namely, gross profit, operating profit, net operating income, profit on ordinary activities before interest, profit on ordinary activities before taxation, profit on ordinary activities after taxation, profit for the financial year and retained profit for the year. Only two of these profit measurers are suitable for use in the present context. They are (a) operating profit and (b) profit on ordinary activities before interest (which is equal to operating profit plus share of profit of associated undertakings). The strength of these measures is that, while taking account (as gross profit does not) of most of the revenues and expenses, they are not affected by interest on loans, dividends on shares, taxation or extraordinary items. If return on investment is to be a satisfactory measure of managerial performance on a continuing basis, it should not be influenced by changes in financial structure (see Chapter 8) or by changes in rates of tax. The advantage of (a) over (b) is that it produces a return on investment measure which is easier to decompose since it does not include the profits of associated undertakings and can therefore be compared with turnover figures which, as we have seen (p. 28), do not include sales made by such companies.

If 'profit' is defined as operating profit or profit before interest, 'net assets' must be defined consistently as total assets less current liabilities (but not long-term liabilities) using either averages or end-of-year figures. Total assets less current liabilities can also be called 'capital employed'. It is equal in amount to shareholders' funds plus long-term liabilities.

In principle, return on investment can be measured in either historical cost or current cost terms. In practice, most companies (British Vita among them) provide only historical cost data, although these are often modified by the revaluation of land and buildings.

All the relevant figures for British Vita for 1993–1997 are set out on p. 6 of its 1997 annual report and p. 72 of its 1996 report. Details of the necessary calculations are given in Tables 6.1 and 6.2.

The tables show turnover increasing each year from 1993 to 1996, the 1996 figure being 28 per cent higher than the 1993 figure. In 1997 turnover fell by 7 per cent, a fall stated by the chief executive as being due, in the main, to the adverse translation effects on sales in overseas subsidiaries caused by the strength of sterling [p. 3]. Operating profit, profit on ordinary activities before interest and taxation, and profit on ordinary activities before interest and taxation as a percentage of average net assets,

Table 6.1. Calculation of Return on Investment, British Vita Group, 1993–97

	Profit on ordinary activities before interest and taxation (a) £m	Net assets (total assets less current liabilities) (b) £m	Average net assets[1] (c) £m	Profit on ordinary activities before interest and taxation as a percentage of average net assets (d) = (a)/(c) × 100 %
1993	32.9	327.4	—	—
1994	48.2	338.6	333.0	14.5
1995	34.8	367.3	352.9	9.9
1996	57.2	342.9	355.1	16.1
1997	65.1	340.3	341.6	19.1

[1] Average net assets for 1997 is equal to the average of net assets 1996 and net assets 1997, and similarly for other years.
Source. British Vita PLC, Annual Report and Accounts, 1997, p. 6; 1996, p. 72.

all increased steadily, apart from a fall-back in 1995, largely due to the size of exceptional and discontinued operations in that year [p. 6] and thus more apparent in Table 6.1 than in Table 6.2.

Table 6.2. Calculation of Operating Profit as Percentage of Turnover, British Vita Group, 1993–97

	Turnover from continuing operations (a) £m	Operating profit before exceptional and discontinued operations (b) £m	Operating profit as a percentage of turnover (c) = (b)/(a) × 100 %
1993	682.0	41.4	6.1
1994	716.0	47.3	6.6
1995	817.8	45.8	5.6
1996	873.5	49.9	5.7
1997	808.4	55.5	6.9

Source. As for Table 6.1.

ANALYSING THE PROFIT AND LOSS ACCOUNT

The details given in the consolidated profit and loss and the notes thereto provide opportunities for further analysis. Table 6.3 sets out turnover, each category of expense and each profit measure for the years 1995 to 1997. The meaning of figures in this 'raw' state is, however, rather difficult to grasp. Table 6.4 therefore expresses all the figures as percentages of turnover. A study of these two tables shows most figures to be fairly stable in percentage terms, with the exception of cost of sales, which has fallen steadily, with a consequent positive effect on the profit figures.

With the help of the segmental analysis supplied in note 1 [p. 28] it is possible to analyse turnover and profitability by class of business (cellular polymers, industrial polymers, fibres and fabrics) and turnover by geographical origin (UK, Continental Europe, international). This is done in Table 6.5, which shows the importance to the group of cellular polymers relative to industrial polymers and fibres and fabrics and of Continental Europe as a market relative to the UK, although the relative Continental

Table 6.3. Turnover, Expenses and Profits, British Vita Group, 1995–97

Year ended 31 December	1995 £m	1996 £m	1997 £m
Turnover	875.6	895.8	808.4
Cost of sales	(697.5)	(697.1)	(612.1)
Gross profit	178.1	198.7	196.3
Distribution costs	(53.8)	(55.6)	(52.1)
Administrative expenses	(92.6)	(94.1)	(88.7)
Operating profit	31.7	49.0	55.5
Share of profits of associated undertakings	6.1	8.3	9.6
Net operating income	37.8	57.3	65.1
Non-operating items	(3.0)	(0.1)	—
Profit on ordinary activities before interest	34.8	57.2	65.1
Net interest receivable	0.9	—	1.1
Profit on ordinary activities before taxation	35.7	57.2	66.2
Tax on profit on ordinary activities	(13.5)	(20.0)	(22.2)
Profit on ordinary activities after taxation	22.2	37.2	44.0
Minority interests	(0.3)	(0.3)	(0.2)
Profit for the financial year	21.9	36.9	43.8

Source. British Vita PLC, Annual Report and Accounts, 1996 and 1997.

European contribution to turnover and profit has been dragged down by the strength of sterling.

Turning back to the profit and loss account as a whole, Table 6.6 shows the way in which each major item – turnover, operating profit, profit on ordinary activities before interest, profit on ordinary activities before taxation and profit for the financial year – increased or decreased in percentage terms in 1996 and 1997. This table confirms what has already been deduced: a recovery in 1996 from poor 1995 figures followed by growth in 1997 except for a fall in turnover.

Table 6.4. Turnover, Expenses and Profits, British Vita Group, 1995–97 (turnover of each year = 100)

Year ended 31 December	1995 %	1996 %	1997 %
Turnover	100	100	100
Cost of sales	80	78	76
Gross profit	20	22	24
Distribution costs	6	6	6
Administrative expenses	11	11	11
Operating profit	4	5	7
Share of profits of associated undertakings	0	1	1
Net operating income	4	6	8
Non-operating items	(0)	(0)	—
Profit on ordinary activities before interest	4	6	8
Net interest receivable	0	0	0
Profit on ordinary activities before taxation	4	6	8
Tax on profit on ordinary activities	(2)	(2)	(3)
Profit on ordinary activities after taxation	3	4	5
Minority interests	(0)	(0)	(0)
Profit for the financial year	3	4	5

Note. Percentages may not add to totals because of rounding.
Source. Based on Table 6.3.

Table 6.5. Segmental Analysis of British Vita's Turnover and Operating Profit 1996–97

Class of business	1996 Turnover		1996 Operating profit		1997 Turnover		1997 Operating profit	
	£m	%	£m	%	£m	%	£m	%
Cellular polymers	505.1	58	27.2	55	459.7	57	32.1	58
Industrial polymers	207.4	24	15.6	31	200.3	25	15.7	28
Fibres and fabrics	161.0	18	7.1	14	148.4	18	7.7	14
	873.5	100	49.9	100	808.4	100	55.5	100
Discontinued activities	22.3		(0.9)		—		—	
	895.8		49.0		808.4		55.5	
Geographical origin								
UK	304.4	35			303.3	38		
Continental Europe	469.2	54			396.4	49		
International	99.9	11			108.7	13		
	873.5	100			808.4	100		
Discontinued activities	22.3				—			
	895.8				808.4	100		

Note. Percentages may not add to totals because of rounding.
Source. British Vita PLC, Annual Report and Accounts, 1997, note 1.

Table 6.6. Growth Rates, British Vita Group, 1996–97

	1996 %	1997 %
Turnover	2.3	(9.8)
Operating profit	54.6	13.3
Profit on ordinary activities before interest	64.4	13.8
Profit on ordinary activities before taxation	60.2	15.7
Profit for the financial year	68.5	18.7

Note. Percentages show percentage increase (decrease) over the previous year (1996 on 1995, 1997 on 1996).
Source. Based on Table 6.3.

Table 6.7. Value Added Statement, British Vita, year ended 31 December 1997

		£m
Turnover[1]		808.4
Bought-in materials and services[2]		544.7
Value added (gross)		263.7
Investment income[3]		3.4
Share of profit of associated undertakings[1]		9.6
Value added available		276.7
Applied as follows:		
To employees[4]		181.1
To providers of capital:		
interest[5]	2.3	
dividends to British Vita shareholders[1]	19.4	
minority share[1]	0.2	
		21.9
To governments as taxation[6]		22.0
To retentions for replacement and expansion:		
depreciation[7]	27.3	
retained profit[1]	24.4	
		51.7
		276.7

[1] As in the consolidated profit and loss account [p. 24]

[2] Balancing figure equal to

		£m
Cost of sales[1]		612.1
Distribution costs[1]		52.1
Administrative expenses[1]		88.7
		752.9
less employment costs [p. 29]	181.1	
depreciation [p. 29]	27.3	
		208.4
		544.5
add government grants [p. 29]		0.2
		544.7

[3] Interest receivable [p. 29]

[4] Employment costs [p. 29]

[5] Interest payable [p. 29]

[6] Taxation in consolidated profit and loss account — 22.2

   less government grants received [p. 29] — (0.1)

[7] As disclosed on [p. 29] — 22.0

CONSTRUCTING A VALUE ADDED STATEMENT

Technically, a statement of value added is merely another way of displaying the figures for a year's operations but with the emphasis on gross value added (i.e., turnover less bought-in materials and services) instead of profit. British Vita's for 1997 can be constructed as in Table 6.7. The notes explain where the figures come from.

ANALYSING THE VALUE ADDED STATEMENT

A number of useful ratios can be calculated from a value added statement. The ratio of value added to turnover, for example, provides a measure of vertical integration – that is, of the extent to which a group of companies produces its own raw materials and distributes its own products as distinct from buying these from outside. The higher the ratio, the greater the extent of vertical integration. British Vita's ratio (263.8 ÷ 808.4 x 100 = 33 per cent) is relatively low. Value added per £1 of employment costs is £1.46 (£263.8m ÷ £181.1m) and value added per employee is £27,742 (£263.8m ÷ 9,509) (In making this calculation the employees of the associated undertakings are excluded [note 9, p. 30].) The more technically advanced an industry, the higher these figures are likely to be. We have already looked in Chapter 2 (p. 16) at the way, expressed in percentage terms, in which the value added is allocated among employees, providers of capital, taxation and retentions.

7   **Liquidity and Cash Flows**

One may not doubt that, somehow, good
Shall come of water and of mud;
And, sure, the reverent eye must see
A purpose in liquidity.

Rupert Brooke, 'Heaven'

LIQUIDITY

It is very important that a company should be profitable; it is just as important that it should be liquid. In particular, companies which are profitable in the long term must make sure that they do not fail through lack of liquidity in the short term. An increase in profits must by definition lead to an increase in a company's net assets. There is no reason, however, why its liquid assets, such as cash in the bank, should automatically increase. A profitable and fast-expanding company may find that it has tied up so much of its profits in fixed assets, stocks and debtors that it has difficulty in paying its debts as they fall due. To help prevent such a situation, a company should prepare a cash budget – that is, a plan of future cash receipts and payments, based on specified assumptions about such things as sales growth, credit terms, issues of shares and expansion of plant. A simple example demonstrating how a profitable company may run into liquidity problems is given below.

Oodnadatta Ltd is formed on 1 January to make boomerangs at a cost of £1.50 each and sell them for £2 each. All bills are paid immediately and debts are collected within thirty days. The stock of boomerangs

Table 7.1. Oodnadatta Ltd, Cash Budget and Budgeted Profit and Loss Statement

Budgeted Profit and Loss Statement

	Jan. £	Feb. £	Mar. £	Apr. £	May £	June £	July £	Aug. £	Sep. £	Oct. £	Nov. £	Dec. £	Total £
Sales	—	800	1,200	1,600	2,000	2,400	2,800	3,200	3,600	4,000	4,400	4,800	30,800
Cost of sales	—	600	900	1,200	1,500	1,800	2,100	2,400	2,700	3,000	3,300	3,600	23,100
Profit	—	200	300	400	500	600	700	800	900	1,000	1,100	1,200	7,700

Note. The sales figures are equal to the quantity sold multiplied by £2; the cost of sales figures to the quantity sold multiplied by £1.50; the profit figures to the quantity sold multiplied by £0.50. Note that the cost of sales figures give the cost of the goods *sold* during the month, *not* the cost of the goods *manufactured* during the month.

Cash Budget

	Jan. £	Feb. £	Mar. £	Apr. £	May £	June £	July £	Aug. £	Sep. £	Oct. £	Nov. £	Dec. £
Balance at beginning of month	+600	—	—900	—1,300	—1,600	—1,800	—1,900	—1,900	—1,800	—1,600	—1,300	—900
Cash received from debtors	—	—	+800	+1,200	+1,600	+2,000	+2,400	+2,800	+3,200	+3,600	+4,000	+4,400
Cash payment to creditors	—600	—900	—1,200	—1,500	—1,800	—2,100	—2,400	—2,700	—3,000	—3,300	—3,600	—3,900
Balance at end of month	—	—900	—1,300	—1,600	—1,800	—1,900	—1,900	—1,800	—1,600	—1,300	—900	—400

Note. Cash received from debtors is equal to the sales of the previous month; cash payments to creditors to the cost of sales of the next month.

manufactured and paid for in January, for example, will be sold in February and the cash proceeds collected in March. The company's provisional plans are to sell 400 boomerangs in February, 600 in March, 800 in April and so on. At 1 January the company has £600 in cash (raised by an issue of shares) – just sufficient to cover the manufacture of the first 400 boomerangs – but no other assets.

Table 7.2. Oodnadatta Ltd, Balance Sheets, 1 January and 31 December

Balance Sheets	1 January £	31 December £	Difference £
Cash	+ 600	− 400	− 1,000
Debtors	—	+ 4,800	+ 4,800
Stocks	—	+ 3,900	+ 3,900
	+ 600	+ 8,300	+ 7,700
Share capital	+ 600	+ 600	—
Retained profits	—	+ 7,700	+ 7,700
	+ 600	+ 8,300	+ 7,700

Note. The cash figure at 31 December is taken from the cash budget; the debtors represent the December sales, the cash for which will not be collected until January; the stocks represent the cost of goods manufactured and paid for in December for sale in January next.

Before actually starting production, the company draws up monthly budgets relating to profits and cash flows (Table 7.1). The figures show that although the planned profit for the year is £7,700, cash will fall by £1,000 from a positive £600 to a negative £400. There is thus £8,700 to be accounted for. We can see what will happen by comparing the balance sheet at 1 January with that which will result at 31 December (Table 7.2). The difference column shows the position quite clearly. All the profits, plus the original cash (£600), plus another £400 are tied up in debtors and stocks. It is interesting to note, however, that by the end of next January the company's liquidity crisis will be over:

	31 January
Balance at beginning of month	− 400
Cash received from debtors	+ 4,800
	+ 4,400
Cash payments to creditors	− 4,200
	£+ 200

The catch is, of course, that, as a result of its 'overtrading', the company is unlikely to reach next January in spite of its excellent profit-making potential, unless it can raise more cash by borrowing, by collecting its debts faster, or by keeping down the size of its stock.

If sales continue to rise and costs also remain the same, the company will run into the opposite problem: excess liquidity. The purpose of drawing up cash budgets is to ensure that a company neither runs out of cash nor keeps cash idle when it could be profitably invested.

CURRENT AND LIQUID RATIOS

British Vita's cash flow statement was discussed in Chapter 2. In 1996 cash increased by £4.7 million; in 1997 it decreased by £2.8 million, in spite of a net increase in loans of £16.3 million. In the remainder of this chapter we will look at several measures of liquidity, taking account of all the current assets, not just cash, and of the current liabilities.

Although cash budgets are an essential part of internal company financial management, they are unavailable to the external financial analyst, who must therefore use rather less precise measures of liquidity. What the analyst tries to do is to approximate the possible future cash flows as closely as possible. One crude measure of liquidity is the relationship between the current assets and current liabilities. This is known as the 'current ratio', and is defined as follows:

$$\text{current ratio} = \frac{\text{current assets}}{\text{current liabilities}}.$$

In calculating both current assets and current liabilities for the purpose of liquidity ratios, care must be taken to exclude any amounts falling due after more than one year. Current ratios can be calculated including or excluding short-term borrowings (including bank overdrafts and medium- and long-term loans which have reached their final year before repayment). The calculations for the British Vita group are explained in Table 7.4.

A more immediate measure of liquidity can be found by excluding stocks from the numerator. The resulting ratio is known as the liquid, quick or acid-test ratio:

$$\text{liquid ratio} = \frac{\text{current assets} - \text{stocks}}{\text{current liabilities}}.$$

The liquid ratio has the incidental advantage of being more easily compared among companies, since it does not depend, as does the current ratio to some extent, on the method chosen to value the stock-in-trade. Many analysts also exclude amounts owed by and owing to associated companies from, respectively, the numerator and denominator of the liquid ratio, and we shall follow this practice. The calculations for British Vita are explained in Table 7.5.

Table 7.3 analyses the composition of the current assets, looking at the relative proportions of stocks, debtors and cash (including short-term investments).

Tables 7.3, 7.4 and 7.5 suggest that the group's liquidity is both satisfactory and stable, with, however, less liquidity in 1996 than in the other two years.

Table 7.3. Composition of Current Assets, British Vita Group, 1995–97

	Total current assets %	Stocks %	Debtors %	Cash and short-term investments %
1995	100	26	55	18
1996	100	26	55	19
1997	100	25	54	20

Source. British Vita PLC, Annual Report and Accounts, 1996 and 1997.

Table 7.4. Calculation of Current Ratios, British Vita Group, 1995–97

	Current assets as reported in balance sheet (a) £m	Current assets excluding debtors falling due after more than one year (b) £m	Current liabilities as reported in balance sheet (c) £m	Current liabilities excluding short-term borrowings (d) £m	Current ratio (e) = (b) ÷ (c)	Current ratio excluding short-term borrowings (f) = (b) ÷ (d)
1995	343.3	339.0	232.4	191.6	1.46	1.77
1996	293.2	291.2	202.5	182.7	1.44	1.59
1997	296.6	294.2	200.9	179.0	1.46	1.64

Source. As for Table 7.3. Percentages may not add to totals because of rounding.

Table 7.5. Calculation of Liquid Ratios, British Vita Group, 1995–97

	Liquid assets (= col. b, Table 7.3, less stocks and amounts owed by associated undertakings) (g) £m	Col. c, Table 7.3, less amounts owing to associated undertakings (h) £m	Col. d, Table 7.3, less amounts owing to associated undertakings (i) £m	Liquid ratio (j) = (g) ÷ (h)	Liquid ratio excluding short-term borrowings (k) = (g) ÷ (i)
1995	247.4	232.3	191.5	1.07	1.29
1996	214.0	202.3	182.5	1.06	1.17
1997	218.3	200.8	178.9	1.09	1.22

Source. As for Table 7.3.

DEFENSIVE OR NO-CREDIT INTERVAL

Both the current ratio and the liquid ratio are static rather than dynamic; that is, they treat liquidity as something to be measured at a point in time rather than over a period. A more dynamic approach would be to divide the liquid assets not by the current liabilities but by those operating expenses which require the use of liquid assets; namely, cost of sales, distribution costs and administrative expenses. Depreciation is not included as it is not a cash expense. What is sought is a crude measure of how long a company could survive without borrowing if no receipts were coming in from debtors. The calculations for British Vita are shown in Table 7.6.

Table 7.6. Calculation of Defensive Intervals, British Vita Group, 1995–97

	Liquid assets (= col. g, Table 7.4) (a) £m	Operating expenses requiring use of liquid assets (cost of sales, distribution costs, administrative expenses, excluding depreciation)(b) £m	Defensive interval (days) (c) = (a) ÷ (b) × 365
1995	247.4	810.3	111
1996	214.0	815.7	96
1997	218.3	725.6	110

Source. As for Table 7.3.

The result of the calculations, measured in days by multiplying the ratio by 365, can be called the 'defensive (or no-credit) interval'.

It would be preferable to use forecast rather than past cash expenses, but these, of course, are not available to the external analyst. The defensive intervals calculated in Table 7.6 confirm the conclusions of the previous calculations, that the group is sufficiently liquid, and that the 1997 ratios have returned to those of 1995.

AVERAGE COLLECTION PERIOD AND STOCK TURNOVER

Another important indicator of liquidity is the speed at which debts are collected. The average collection period for debtors can be calculated as follows, if one assumes that all sales are for credit:

$$\frac{\text{trade debtors} \times 365}{\text{sales}} \text{ days.}$$

Average debtors (defined as the mean of the opening and closing debtors figures) are also sometimes used. One problem with this ratio is that debtors include value added tax (VAT), whereas sales do not.

Another way of looking at the average collection period would be to think in terms of debtors turnover: $\frac{\text{sales}}{\text{average debtors}}$. The relationship between stocks and cost of sales is usually looked at in this way: stock turnover $= \frac{\text{cost of sales}}{\text{stocks}}$. In assessing these ratios, it must be remembered that they are weighted averages. There are important differences per class of business and per geographical area which only more detailed accounts would reveal.

Table 7.7 shows how British Vita's average collection period and stock turnover can be calculated. The sales (= turnover) and cost of sales figures are taken from the consolidated profit and loss accounts and the stocks figures from the consolidated balance sheet. Trade debtors are taken from the notes relating to debtors.

Table 7.7. Calculation of Average Collection Period and Stock Turnover, British Vita Group, 1995–97

	Sales (a) £m	Trade debtors (b) £m	Cost of sales (c) £m	Stocks (d) £m	Average collection period (b) ÷ (a) × 365 days	Stock turnover (c) ÷ (d)
1995	875.6	158.2	697.5	90.8	66	7.7
1996	895.8	140.5	697.1	76.4	57	9.1
1997	808.4	140.8	612.1	75.1	64	8.2

Source. As for Table 7.3.

The average collection period relates to credit taken. A similar calculation for credit given can be made as follows:

$$\frac{\text{trade creditors} \times 365}{\text{purchases}} \text{ days.}$$

Table 7.8 shows how the average payment period for British Vita is calculated. Trade creditors are taken from the note relating to creditors. Purchases are approximated by adjusting the cost of sales by the change in the raw materials and consumable stores [note 13, p. 35]. British Vita sets out its creditors payments policy in the Directors' Report [p. 18].

Table 7.8. Calculation of Average Payment Period, British Vita Group, 1995–97

	Purchases (a) £m	Trade creditors (b) £m	Average payment period (b) ÷ (a) × 365 days
1995	697.5	116.2	61
1996	687.4	99.7	53
1997	611.8	99.6	59

Source. As for Table 7.3.

Tables 7.7 and 7.8 provide further evidence that 1996 is the odd year out, with average collection and payment periods lower than in the other two years and stock turnover higher. In all years average collection periods are longer than average payment periods.

PREDICTING INSOLVENCY

The extreme case of illiquidity is insolvency, which occurs when a company is unable to pay its debts as they fall due.

Can financial ratios be used to predict insolvency in advance? Researchers in both the USA and the UK have approached this problem by examining the ratios of companies just prior to their insolvency. It is possible by the use of statistical techniques to calculate what is known as a

'Z-score' for companies based on a number of relevant ratios appropriately weighted. Companies with scores within a certain range are more likely to become insolvent.

As is usual in ratio analysis, it is necessary to use more than one ratio and the result is a guide, not a certainty. A company with a bad score is not certain to become insolvent, but only more likely to.

WINDOW-DRESSING

We end this chapter with an illustration of a problem which arises from the nature of ratios, and can give rise to a form of creative accounting. Suppose that a company has current assets of £800,000, current liabilities of £500,000 and liquid assets of £550,000. Its *net* current assets and *net* liquid assets will therefore be £300,000 and £50,000 respectively. If we keep these *net* amounts constant but vary the gross figures using current assets to pay off current liabilities, then the current and liquid ratios will vary as shown in Table 7.9.

Table 7.9. Illustration of Window-dressing

Current assets (a) £000	Current liabilities (b) £000	Liquid assets (c) £000	Current ratio (a) ÷ (b)	Liquid ratio (c) ÷ (b)
800	500	550	1.60	1.10
700	400	450	1.75	1.12
600	300	350	2.00	1.17
500	200	250	2.50	1.25
400	100	150	4.00	1.50
350	50	100	7.00	2.00
301	1	51	301.00	51.00

This is one example of window-dressing, which may be defined more generally as any transaction, the purpose of which is to so arrange affairs that the financial statements of a company give a misleading or unrepresentative impression of its financial position. The example is exaggerated to make a point, but it is important to note that, within limits, companies may be able to arrange their current assets and liabilities so as to have the desired ratios at balance sheet time.

8 Sources of Funds and Capital Structure

Les affaires, c'est bien simple: c'est l'argent des autres.

Alexandre Dumas, fils, *La Question d'argent*

SOURCES OF FUNDS

The funds available to a company are obtained either from its shareholders or by borrowing. The former includes not only issues of shares but also the retention of profits. The latter range from long-term debt to trade credit. The composition at any time of these sources, and more especially the long-term sources, is referred to as the 'capital structure' of a company. For most companies the most important source of funds is the ordinary shareholders, especially through the medium of reserves (which consist mainly of retained profits), but also through the issue of new shares. Preference shares and minority interests are of small importance. Loans are important, although usually well behind reserves. Provisions for liabilities and charges (which include deferred taxation and pensions) are also quite important.

The sources of funds of the British Vita group are disclosed in the balance sheets, the cash flow statement and the relevant notes. The reliance on shareholders' funds is very clear. At 31 December 1996 and 1997 the group balance sheets [p. 26] disclose that the total assets less current liabilities of £342.9 million (1996) and £340.3 million (1997) have been financed as follows:

	1996		1997	
	£m	%	£m	%
Shareholders' funds	298.0	87	286.1	84
Borrowings	19.0	6	30.1	9
Provisions for liabilities and charges	22.2	6	18.7	6
Minority interests	1.0	0	1.1	0
Other creditors	2.7	1	4.3	1
	342.9	100	340.3	100

Compared with 1996, there was a slight increase, both absolute and relative, in borrowings in 1997.

CAPITAL STRUCTURE

Is there such a thing as an optimal capital structure for a particular company? This is a question which has aroused much debate. In principle there probably is such a structure, but it is not simple in practice for a company either to discover what it is or to achieve it.

The main problem is to choose the best mix of debt (loans, debentures) and equity (ordinary shares, reserves, retained profits). There is no easy way of doing this. It is possible to list the factors which ought to be considered, but assessing the weight to be given to each remains very largely a matter of judgement and experience. The factors are:

1. *Cost*. The current and future cost of each potential source of capital should be estimated and compared. It should be borne in mind that costs of each source are not necessarily independent of each other. An increase in debt now, for example, may push up the cost of equity later. Other things being equal, it is desirable to minimize the average overall cost of capital to the company.

2. *Risk*. It is unwise (and often disastrous) to place a company in a position where it may be unable, if profits fall even temporarily, to pay interest as it falls due or to pay back loans. It is also undesirable to be forced to cut or omit the ordinary dividend (see the section below on dividend policy).

3. *Control*. Except where there is no alternative, a company should not

make any issue of shares which will have the effect of removing or diluting control by the existing shareholders.

4. *Acceptability*. A company can only borrow if others are willing to lend to it. Few listed companies can afford the luxury of a capital structure which is unacceptable to financial institutions. A company with readily mortgageable assets will find it easier to raise debt.

5. *Transferability*. Shares may be listed or unlisted. Many companies have made issues of shares to the public in order to obtain a Stock Exchange listing and to improve the transferability of their shares. Such a procedure may also have tax advantages.

Cost of capital and risk are discussed in more detail in the next two sections.

COST OF CAPITAL

Although a company cannot always choose what appears to be the cheapest source of capital, because of the need to pay attention to risk, control, acceptability and transferability, it should always estimate the cost of each potential source and the effect on the overall average cost.

A rather oversimplified approach is to work out first of all the cost of each potential source of capital. This is most easily done in the case of debentures. Suppose that a company can issue £100,000 10 per cent debentures at par, repayable at par in twenty years' time. The before-tax cost is obviously 10 per cent; the after-tax cost, assuming immediate payment and a corporation tax rate of 30 per cent, is 7 per cent. If preference shares are issued instead, the before- and after-tax rates would be equal, since preference dividends, unlike debenture interest, are not deductible for tax purposes. This explains why, since the introduction of corporation tax in 1965, many companies have replaced their preference share capital by loan stock.

The arithmetic becomes rather more difficult if the loan stock is not issued at par. Suppose, for example, an issue made in 1991 of £40 million 10.75 per cent unsecured loan stock 2016 at £98 per cent. That is, for every £98 received in 1991 a company promises to pay interest of £10.75

each year and to repay the stock at par (£100) in 2016. It can be calculated that the yield to the redemption date is about 11 per cent.

The real cost of issuing debentures is reduced during a period of inflation by the fact that the cash paid out by the company will be of lower purchasing power than the cash it receives at the date of issue.

Reckoning the cost of an issue of ordinary shares is more difficult. An analogous calculation to the one above would suggest that the cost is equal to the gross dividend yield, worked out as follows:

$$\frac{\text{current dividend per ordinary share} \times 100}{\text{market price per share}} \times \frac{100}{80}.$$

The purpose of multiplying by 100/80 is to allow for a tax credit of 20 per cent.

Dividend yields may be most easily found from the stock exchange pages of the *Financial Times* and other newspapers. The *Financial Times* Share Information Service gives quite a lot of information about shares every day. The following typical entry has been extracted from the *Financial Times* of 27 May 1998 (referring to the day before):

	Price	+ or −	52 week high	low	Yield gross	P/E
British Vita	342	+$^1/_2$	342	196	3.2	17.3

This tells us (for the date in question) that the current market price of British Vita's ordinary shares (par value 25 p) is 342 p, compared with a high for the last 52 weeks of 342 p, a low of 196 p and a price the day before of 341$^1/_2$ p. (Par values may be assumed to be 25 p unless the *Financial Times* states otherwise.)

British Vita's dividend yield (gross) is calculated by the *Financial Times* as follows:

$$\frac{\text{current dividend per ordinary share} \times 100}{\text{market price per share}} \times \frac{100}{80}.$$

That is to say, given the 1997 dividend of 8.75 p per share [p. 1]:

$$\frac{8.75 \times 100}{342} \times \frac{100}{80} = 3.2\%.$$

The dividend yield of any company can be compared with dividend yields in general and with those of other companies in the same equity group or sub-section, by looking at the table in the *Financial Times* headed 'FTSE – Actuaries Share Indices'. On 26 May 1998 the dividend yield for 'Chemicals' was 3.05 per cent.

These yields can be contrasted with the 7.20 per cent yield on irredeemable government securities reported in the same issue of the *Financial Times*. Given the relative riskiness of fixed-interest and variable-dividend securities, this is at first sight surprising. Before August 1959, in fact, the average dividend yield was higher than the yield on government stocks. Since then a 'reverse yield gap', as it is called, has existed. The main reason for the reverse yield gap is the realization by investors that equities offer more protection against the effects of inflation. This has raised share prices relatively and lowered yields.

The dividend yield cannot, however, be regarded as an adequate measure of the cost of equity capital. It fails to take account of the facts that future dividends may be different from the current dividend and that the price of the shares may change. Neither of these considerations is relevant to long-term debt with its fixed interest payments and fixed redemption prices.

Two possible measures of the cost of equity capital are the *earnings yield* and the *dividend yield plus a growth rate*. The earnings yield is calculated as follows:

$$\frac{\text{earnings per ordinary share after tax} \times 100}{\text{market price per ordinary share}}.$$

It is more usual to express the same relationship in the form of a *price-earnings ratio* (P/E ratio), which is simply the reciprocal of the earnings yield multiplied by 100; that is:

$$\frac{\text{market price per ordinary share}}{\text{earnings per ordinary share after tax}}.$$

In other words, the P/E ratio expresses the multiple of the last reported earnings that the market is willing to pay for the ordinary shares. The higher the P/E ratio (the lower the earnings yield), the more the market thinks of the company and the cheaper the cost of equity capital to the company. From the extract from the *Financial Times* it can be seen that British Vita's price–earnings ratio on 27 May 1998 was 17.3. How this calculation was arrived at is explained below.

As already noted, earnings are calculated after the deduction of tax and preference dividends. The tax charge, however, depends to some extent on the dividends declared, since there are both constant and variable components in the charge.

There is a distinction between the 'net basis' and the 'nil basis'. The former takes account of both constant and variable components and has the obvious advantage that all the relevant facts are considered. The latter takes account only of the constant components (i.e., it in effect assumes a nil distribution of dividends). Its advantage is that it produces an EPS which is independent of the level of dividend distribution. For most companies the two bases will in practice give the same result. This is not likely to be the case, however, for companies relying heavily on overseas income. The *Financial Times* calculates P/E ratios on a net basis.

The 1997 calculation [note 8, p. 30] for British Vita is as follows:

$$EPS = \frac{\text{profit for the financial year less preference dividends}}{\text{weighted average of ordinary shares in issue during year}}$$

$$= \frac{£43.8m \times 100}{£221.2m} = 19.8 \text{ p.}$$

The P/E ratio on 26 May 1998 was therefore:

$$\frac{\text{market price per share}}{EPS} = \frac{342}{19.8} = 17.3.$$

Companies also publish a 'fully diluted' EPS figure. Dilution can arise from the existence of shares that may rank for dividend in the future, from convertible preference shares and loan stock, and from options and warrants (see below). British Polythene PLC, for example, reported in 1997 a basic EPS of 41.21 p and a fully diluted EPS, after taking account of the assumed exercise of options over ordinary shares, of 40.37 p.

Earnings are defined in the accounting standard (FRS 14) to include all items of profit and loss including those of both a capital and a revenue nature. The Accounting Standards Board recognizes that companies may wish to publish EPS figures based on other, less inclusive measures of earnings (e.g., excluding items not related to trading performance) and a number of companies do this. British Vita discloses both an all-inclusive EPS and an EPS excluding exceptional items and discontinued operations, expressing a preference for the latter. In 1996, but not in 1997, the two calculations produced different figures [p. 30]. The Institute of Investment Management and Research (IIMR) favours an EPS calculation based on 'headline earnings', which excludes items such as exceptional gains on the sale of fixed assets. The *Financial Times* bases its ratios on headline earnings.

The relationship between EPS and dividend per share (DPS) is known as the dividend cover. In its annual report [p. 4], British Vita reports its dividend cover for 1997 as 2.3, calculated as:

$$\frac{EPS}{DPS} = \frac{19.8}{8.75} = 2.3.$$

Since the market is interested in future dividends, it prefers to see current dividends reasonably well covered by current earnings. This is some sort of guarantee that the dividends will be at least maintained in future since, if profits fall, there will be past retained profits to draw upon.

An alternative approach to the cost of equity capital is to add a growth rate to the dividend yield. If one considers, for example, that British Vita's dividends are likely to grow in future at an average annual rate of 5 per cent, then the cost of its equity capital would be estimated to be 3.2 per cent plus 5 per cent, which equals 8.2 per cent.

An approach to the cost of a company's equity capital strongly favoured in the literature on financial theory is that it is equal to:

$$R_f + \beta[E(R_m) - R_f]$$

where R_f is the return on a riskless security (e.g., a treasury bill), $E(R_m)$ is the expected return on all the securities in the market and ß (beta) is a measure of risk.

The meaning and measurement of beta are discussed in the next section.

RISK: BETAS AND GEARING

Risk is of two kinds: market (or systematic) risk and specific (or non-market) risk. Market risk can be quantified as the beta of a company's ordinary shares. Beta measures the sensitivity of the share price to movements in the market. British Vita's beta was estimated by the London Business School Risk Measurement Service (RMS) (July–September 1998 issue) to be 1.12. A beta of 1.12 means that the share will on average move 1.12 per cent for each 1 per cent move by the market. A share with a beta of 1.0 would on average move in line with the market. Betas as reported in the RMS ranged from 1.67 to 0.04. The beta of the National Westminster Bank, for example, was 1.15. Industry betas are also available: 0.82 for chemicals, advanced materials, and 1.16 for retail banks, if the component companies are equally weighted.

Specific risk refers to factors specific to a company and is measured as a percentage return per annum. The higher the percentage, the greater the specific risk. Investment trusts (companies which invest in the securities of other companies) tend to have the lowest specific risk. Specific risk figures ranged from 221 per cent down to 5 per cent. British Vita's and National Westminster's figures were 26 per cent and 17 per cent respectively. The industry figures were 28 per cent and 22 per cent on an equally weighted basis.

The distinction between market risk and specific risk is important because it is possible to reduce the latter by diversification (e.g., by holding shares in both chemical manufacturers and in retail banks), but market risk cannot be diversified away. Both British Vita and National Westminster are affected by the state of the economy in which they operate.

Betas can be measured from either market data ('market betas') or from accounting data ('accounting betas'). Betas do, of course, change over time, although most are reasonably stationary.

The more traditional accounting measure of risk is gearing. Companies with the highest betas tend to be highly geared and to come from highly cyclical industries.

Gearing (or 'leverage', as the Americans call it) is the relationship between the funds provided to a company by its ordinary shareholders and the long-term sources of funds carrying a fixed interest charge or dividend (e.g., unsecured loans, debentures and preference shares). The degree of gearing can be measured in terms of either capital or income. A company's capital structure is said to be highly geared when the fixed charges claim an above-average proportion of the company's resources of either capital or income.

There are several ways of defining and calculating a 'gearing ratio' and it is always important to know which definition is being used. Whichever way the calculations are made, some companies are likely to be more highly geared than others, especially those which have relatively stable profits, and those which have assets which can be specifically identified and are not expected to fall in value over time, thereby providing good security. One definition of the ratio is:

$$\frac{\text{interest-bearing liabilities } + \text{ preference shares}}{\text{ordinary shareholders' funds}} \times 100\%.$$

British Vita's interest-bearing liabilities are most easily defined as its borrowings falling due after more than one year. This figure as at 31 December 1997 is given in note 17 [p. 37] as £30.1 million. There are no preference shares. The calculation is therefore

$$\frac{30.1}{286.1} \times 100 = 11\%.$$

A similar calculation for 1996 (allowing for the preference shares) produces a gearing ratio of 6 per cent. Gearing has increased because, as noted at the beginning of this chapter, borrowings have increased and ordinary shareholders' funds decreased.

British Vita itself calculates gearing by the net cash method, where 'net cash' is defined as cash at bank and short-term investments less borrowings (falling due within one year and after more than one year). At 31 December 1997 this figure was £8 million (i.e., £60.0 − £21.9 − £30.1). The net cash ratio is the ratio of net cash to shareholders' funds and will be negative if cash exceeds borrowings. A higher positive percentage and a lower negative percentage shows an increase in gearing. At 31 December 1997 it is calculated as:

$$\frac{(8.0) \times 100}{286.1} = -3\%.$$

Table 8.1 shows British Vita's gearing ratio and net cash ratio from 1995 to 1997. The two ratios may on occasion give conflicting signals but both suggest an increase in gearing in 1997 compared with 1996. By comparison with most companies, British Vita's gearing is low.

Table 8.1. British Vita PLC: Gearing Ratio and Net Cash Ratio, 1995–97

	Gearing Ratio %	Net Cash Ratio %
1995	6	(2)
1996	6	(5)
1997	11	(3)

Source. British Vita PLC, Annual Report and Accounts, 1997, page 6.

All the above definitions are based on book values. Market values could (some would say 'should') be used instead if they are available. Our original definition would then become:

$$\frac{\text{market value of fixed interest securities}}{\text{market value of ordinary share capital}}.$$

'Times interest earned' is a different way of looking at gearing based on the profit and loss account rather than the balance sheet. It is defined as:

$$\frac{\text{profit before interest and tax}}{\text{interest (gross of tax)}}.$$

The lower this ratio, the more highly geared a company is; that is, the worse the cover for interest payments.

Using the data on p. 6 of the 1997 report and adjusting for interest received [note 5, p. 29], times interest earned can be calculated for British Vita as follows:

$$1996 \quad \frac{57.2}{2.6} = 22 \text{ times}$$

$$1997 \quad \frac{65.1}{2.3} = 28 \text{ times}$$

This measure shows British Vita becoming less highly geared in 1997.

The major disadvantage of the 'times interest earned' method is that it ignores the existence of reserves; that is, the retained profits of previous years, upon which the company could call if necessary (if they are in liquid form). The same drawback applies to the 'priority percentages' approach, in which the analyst calculates the percentage of earnings that is required to service each category of loan and share capital.

The effect of gearing on profits available to ordinary shareholders can be seen from the following example.

X PLC is a very highly geared company and Y PLC a relatively low geared one. Their long-term sources of funds at the beginning of the year are as follows:

	X	Y
Ordinary share capital (par value)	100,000	200,000
Retained profit	100,000	200,000
Ordinary shareholders' funds	200,000	400,000
10% debenture	300,000	100,000
	£ 500,000	£ 500,000
Gearing ratio (debentures as percentage of ordinary shareholders' funds)	150%	25%

If profit before interest and tax during the year is £80,000 for both companies, the distributable profit will be as follows, assuming a 30 per cent tax rate:

	X	Y
(a) Profit before interest and tax	80,000	80,000
(b) Debenture interest (gross)	30,000	10,000
	50,000	70,000
Tax at 30%	15,000	21,000
	35,000	49,000
Times interest earned (a ÷ b)	2.67	8.00

Distributable profit will be 35 per cent of the par value for Company X and 24.5 per cent for Company Y.

If, however, the profit before interest and tax is £160,000, the position will be as follows:

	X	Y
(a) Profit before interest and tax	160,000	160,000
(b) Debenture interest (gross)	30,000	10,000
	130,000	150,000
Tax at 30%	39,000	45,000
	91,000	105,000
Times interest earned (a ÷ b)	5.33	16.00

Distributable profit as a proportion of the par value becomes 91 per cent for Company X and 52.5 per cent for Company Y. Note that while profits before interest and tax have doubled, X's distributable profit as a percentage of par value has gone up 2.60 times and Y's 2.14 times (because Y is less highly geared than X). It is clear that gearing enables a company to trade on the equity, as the Americans say, and to increase the ordinary shareholders' return at a faster rate than the increase in profits. The higher the gearing, the greater the relative rate.

Unfortunately, the converse also applies. Suppose that the profit before interest and tax falls to £30,000. The position will then be as follows:

	X	Y
(a) Profit before interest and tax	30,000	30,000
(b) Debenture interest (gross)	30,000	10,000
	—	20,000
Tax at 30%	—	6,000
Distributable profit	—	14,000
Times interest earned (a ÷ b)	1.00	3.00

The distributable profit as a proportion of par value of Company X falls to zero and that of Company Y to 7 per cent. If profits fell even further, Company X would not be able to pay the debenture interest out of its current profits. Company Y is in a much better position to meet such an emergency. It must also be remembered, of course, that a company which has tied up its assets too much in fixed assets and stocks may run into similar problems even though its profits have not fallen. Profits are not the same thing as ready cash.

The moral is that companies whose profits are low or likely to fluctuate violently should not be too highly geared. Investors in such companies are running risks and will in any case prefer ordinary shares to fixed-interest debentures. From a company point of view the attraction of a relatively cheap source of funds must be balanced against the risks involved.

DIVIDEND POLICY

How does a company determine the size of the dividend it pays each year, or, putting the same question round the other way, how does a company decide how much of its profits to retain each year?

Retained profits are the most convenient source of funds, and a company which pays very high dividends loses this source and may have to raise money in the capital market. Issues of debentures and other loans usually have a lower cost of capital than either new issues of shares or retained profits, but, as we have just seen, there are dangers in a too highly geared capital structure. New issues of shares are more expensive than retained profits because of the issue costs involved.*

On the other hand, most expanding companies will have to go to the market sooner or later, and one of the points that potential investors will look at is the dividend record. A company whose dividend has declined or fluctuated violently is not likely to be favourably regarded. For this reason companies prefer to maintain their dividends even if earnings fall. Dividends have an information content; that is, they alter or confirm investors' beliefs about the future prospects of a company.

On the whole, then, cost of capital considerations push companies towards constant or steadily increasing dividend payouts. Inflation may have the same effect if the directors of a company feel that the distribution to shareholders ought to keep pace with the decline in the purchasing power of money. It may also have the opposite effect if the directors feel the need to retain a higher proportion of historical cost earnings in order to maintain operating capacity. Two other factors which may affect the size of the dividend are government policy and taxation. A number of governments since the Second World War, although not recently, in

---

* Retained profits are not a costless source of funds. They can be regarded as a notional distribution of profits which are immediately reinvested in the company.

their efforts to contain rises in wages and prices, have placed statutory limitations on the size of company dividends. In spite of capital gains tax, the British tax system still favours capital increases rather than income increases. There are many shareholders who are more interested in capital gains than dividends. Institutional shareholders with charitable status have been able to reclaim the tax credits attached to dividends received. With the removal of this concession, they may exert pressure for higher dividend payouts. In general, shareholders are likely to be attracted to companies which have a dividend policy suited to their needs. This is known as the 'clientele effect'.

Table 8.2. British Vita PLC: Earnings and Dividends Record, 1993–97

	1993	1994	1995	1996	1997
Profit for the financial year (£m)	20.6	32.0	21.9	36.9	43.8
Index (1993 = 100)	100	155	106	179	213
Earnings per ordinary share[1]	9.6 p	14.7 p	10.0 p	16.8 p	19.8 p
Ordinary dividend (£m)	15.7	16.6	17.3	18.0	19.4
Index (1993 = 100)	100	106	110	115	124
Dividend per ordinary share[1]	7.4 p	7.7 p	7.95 p	8.25 p	8.75 p
Dividend cover	1.3	1.9	1.3	2.0	2.3
Index of retail prices (average for calendar year)	141	144	149	153	157

[1] Adjusted for capitalization and rights issues.
Sources. British Vita PLC, Annual Report and Accounts, 1997; Table 4.2 above.

We are now in a position to look at British Vita's dividend policy. Table 8.2 gives information about the group's dividend policy for the last five years. It has been adapted from the information given on p. 6 of the 1997 Report. It is interesting to compare the earnings record with the dividend record. Profit for the financial year and EPS fluctuated considerably, whereas both dividends and DPS rose steadily throughout the period. In line with the practices of many companies, British Vita's policy has been to keep dividends rising steadily in money terms despite fluctuations in profits. As a result of this policy, the dividend cover also varied over the period. A comparison of DPS and the retail price index shows that for the period 1993 to 1997 the former increased by 18 per cent, the latter by 11 per cent; that is, dividends per share rose in real as well as money terms.

RIGHTS ISSUES AND CAPITALIZATION ISSUES

Most issues of shares are either rights issues or capitalization issues. A rights issue is one in which existing shareholders are given a chance to subscribe before anybody else. If they do not wish to do so, they can sell their rights on the market. Rights issues have long been the norm, and since 1980 it has been obligatory for share issues by public companies to be rights issues unless the shareholders pass a resolution to the contrary.

British Vita last made a rights issue in 1992, offering 35,416,471 new ordinary shares of 25 p each on the basis of one new ordinary share for every five ordinary shares held on 4 March 1992. The offer price, fixed as usual a little below the current market price, was 212 p per share.

The effect of the rights issue on British Vita's balance sheet (ignoring the issue costs) was as follows:

	£m
Increase in cash balances (35,416,471 × 212 p)	75.083
Represented by	
increase in share capital (at par) (35,416,471 × 25 p)	8.854
increase in share premium (35,416,471 × 187 p)	66.229
	75.083

The purpose of the issue was announced by the board of directors to be to provide for future acquisitions and investments.

A capitalization issue (also known as a 'scrip issue' or a 'bonus issue') is simply a means of turning reserves into share capital. To clear up the misunderstandings which can arise from this, it is helpful to use a simple example. Consider a company whose summarized balance sheet is as follows:

Assets	150,000	Ordinary share capital (40,000 shares of £1 each)	40,000
less			
Liabilities	50,000	Reserves	60,000
	£100,000		£100,000

The company decides to make a capitalization issue of one new share for two old shares. The balance sheet will now look like this:

Assets	150,000	Ordinary share capital (60,000 shares of £1 each)	60,000
less			
Liabilities	50,000	Reserves	40,000
	£100,000		£100,000

All that happened is a book entry. In order to increase the ordinary share capital from £40,000 to £60,000, the accountant has decreased the reserves from £60,000 to £40,000. The shareholders have not received any cash, only more paper. Are they any better off? In principle, no; the market price *per share* might be expected to fall proportionately. It may not do so, partly because unrelated factors may be affecting share prices at the same time, partly because the issue may have drawn favourable attention to the future prospects of the company. Of course, if the company announces at the same time that the total amount to be paid out in dividends to shareholders will be increased, then the shareholders really will receive more cash in future.

Capitalization issues have to be adjusted for when making comparisons of earnings per share (EPS). In this example, if the earnings were £12,000 the EPS before the capitalization issue would be 30 p; after the issue it would be 20 p.

British Vita used part of its share premium in 1990 to make a capitalization issue; 57,966,003 ordinary shares of 25 p par value were allotted to existing shareholders fully paid, decreasing the share premium account (an undistributable reserve) by approximately £14.492 million and increasing share capital by the same amount.

CONVERTIBLE LOAN STOCK, OPTIONS AND WARRANTS

So far in this book we have drawn a rather rigid dividing line between debenture-holders, who are merely long-term creditors of a company, and shareholders, who are its owners. It will have been apparent, however, that preference share capital has some of the characteristics of long-term debt. Another hybrid security of importance is the convertible loan.

The 1997 annual report of City Site Estates PLC, for example, includes the following item among the long-term loan capital: '7% convertible unsecured loan stock 2005/06'. The attraction of such stock to investors is that it enables them to buy a fixed-interest stock which they can later change into ordinary shares if they so wish. Whether they will make the conversion or not depends, of course, on the relationship between the market price of the ordinary shares and the conversion price at the conversion date. The investors' hope is that they have found a cheaper way of buying the ordinary shares than direct purchase. The disadvantage is that the rate of interest offered on a convertible loan is less than that on a 'straight' loan.

Why should a company issue convertible stock? There are at least two possibilities:

1. The company wants to issue debt and adds the convertibility as an added attraction.
2. The company would prefer to issue equity but feels that the price of its ordinary shares is temporarily depressed. By setting the conversion price higher than the current price, the management can, if its expectations are fulfilled, effectively make a share issue at the desired price.

The possible disadvantages to the company are that either the market price fails to rise and it is saddled with unwanted debt, or that the market price rises so quickly that it finds itself in effect selling equity more cheaply than it need have done. As already noted, the existence of convertible loan stock dilutes the basic earnings per share.

An option is a contract giving a right to buy or sell securities within or at the end of a given time period at an agreed price. Convertible loan stock is thus one form of option, as are also warrants (certificates giving the holder the right to purchase a security at a predetermined price at a future date or dates). British Vita, like most listed companies, grants options in its shares to both its directors and its employees. Details are given in note 20 [pp. 39–40].

LEASING

Instead of borrowing money to buy fixed assets, a company may decide to lease them; that is, to enter into a contract which allows it the use of the assets (but does not give it the ownership) in return for a periodic rental. Early termination of the lease is penalized. Sometimes the company already owns the assets and raises cash by selling them and then leasing them back. This is known as sale-and-leaseback.

If the lease is for a long period, the effect in either case is similar to an issue of long-term debt, and it should be regarded and analysed as such. It is standard accounting practice for finance leases (leases that transfer substantially all the risks and rewards of ownership to the lessee) to be capitalized. This means that both the leased asset and the long-term liability to pay the lease rentals are shown in the balance sheet. Leases that do not transfer substantially all the risks and rewards of ownership to the lessee are termed operating leases and are not capitalized. Hiring and leasing charges have to be disclosed in the notes. British Vita discloses a figure of £3.1 million in 1997 [note 3, p. 29]. The accounting treatment of leases by the group is also explained [p. 22].

OFF BALANCE SHEET FINANCING

Off balance sheet financing is the funding of a company's operations in such a way that under legal requirements and accounting standards some or all of the finance is not disclosed in its balance sheet. One effect of this will be to make a company look less highly geared than it really is. Off balance sheet financing obviously has the potential to mislead users of financial statements. It has been achieved in many ingenious ways, although the ASB has done its best to limit it by the promulgation of, *inter alia*, FRS 4 (Capital instruments) and of FRS 5 (Reporting the substance of transactions).

Two examples will illustrate the techniques used and how the ASB has sought to combat them. If a subsidiary issues redeemable preference shares with a dividend equal to current interest rates, it could be argued that the preference shares should be shown in the *consolidated* balance sheet as minority interest, not debt. However, FRS 4 requires that where payment of the dividends has been guaranteed by another member of the group, it should be recorded as debt in the consolidated balance sheet. A second example is the sale of goods by a company to a bank with a commitment or option to repurchase them at a *higher* amount. The form of this transaction relates solely to sales and purchases and to the profit and loss account, but it could be argued that the substance is a bank loan, especially if, as may be the case, the goods do not change their physical location, and FRS 5 requires this treatment.

Summary and Reading Guide

The reader who has come this far has already learned a great deal about the annual reports of companies, about financial statements and about accounting and finance. The purpose of this chapter is to summarize what has been learned and to make suggestions about further reading.

COMPANIES

Chapter 1 was mainly about companies, the most important form of business organization in modern Britain. About 99 per cent of all companies are private, but public companies (or groups headed by them) are of greater economic significance. It is with public companies, and especially with those that are listed on the Stock Exchange, that investors are mainly concerned. Published annual reports are typically those of groups of companies, consisting of a parent company, subsidiaries, sub-subsidiaries and associated undertakings.

Companies operate within the legal framework of the Companies Act 1985 and relevant case law. There are many good textbooks on company law. The most readable, although not the shortest, is P. L. Davies and D. Prentice, *Gower's Principles of Modern Company Law* (Sweet & Maxwell, 6th edn, 1997).

FINANCIAL STATEMENTS

Chapter 2 dealt with financial statements. The three most important statements are:

1. *The balance sheet*, which shows the assets, the liabilities and the shareholders' funds at a particular date.
2. *The profit and loss account* (or income statement), which shows for an accounting period the revenues, expenses, net profit (before and after taxation) and often also the distribution of the profit.
3. *The cash flow statement*, which shows the cash flows of a company over the same accounting period.

Assets are classified into *fixed* and *current*, and liabilities classified according to whether they fall due within one year or more than one year. The excess of current assets over current liabilities is the working capital of a company. Tangible fixed assets are depreciated over their estimated economic lives, depreciation in its accounting sense normally referring to the allocation over time of the cost less estimated scrap value. Intangible assets such as goodwill and brands have increased in importance in recent years.

Long-term sources of funds of companies can be divided into *loans and other borrowings* (including debentures) on the one hand and *shareholders' funds* (share capital and reserves) on the other. There is an important distinction between preference shares, usually carrying a fixed dividend rate and having priority in a winding up, and ordinary shares. The par or face value of a share is not necessarily the same as its issue price (issues are often made at a premium) or its market price.

The profit and loss account is drawn up from the point of view of the shareholders and discloses items such as turnover, cost of sales, gross profit, operating profit, profit on ordinary activities before interest, profit on ordinary activities before and after taxation, profit for the financial year and retained profit for the financial year. The same underlying data can be used to prepare a statement of value added, which shows how much wealth has been created by the operations of the group and how that wealth has been allocated.

The cash flow statement demonstrates among other things the difference between increases in profit and increases in cash balances. Cash flow is a rather imprecise term, sometimes meaning simply net profit plus depreciation and other items not involving the movement of funds.

A good introductory book on accounting and financial statements is C. Nobes, *Introduction to Financial Accounting* (International Thomson, 4th edn, 1997). At a more advanced and detailed level, the latest edition of M. Davies, R. Paterson and A. Wilson, *UK GAAP* (Macmillan, for Ernst & Young) is invaluable.

TAXATION

Chapter 3 dealt mainly with taxation and audit. Companies pay corporation tax, not income tax. Taxable income is measured in a somewhat similar way to accounting profit, with the major exception of capital allowances (which replace depreciation). The corporation tax rate refers to a financial year which ends on 31 March, but companies are assessed on the basis of their own accounting periods.

Under the UK's imputation system, shareholders receive a tax credit when a dividend is paid.

In general, taxable income has tended to be less than accounting profit. The total amount of taxation so 'deferred' is disclosed in the notes but only included in the balance sheet to the extent that it is regarded as a liability.

Books on taxation tend to be written either for accountants (lots of figures), for lawyers (lots of case law) or for economists (lots of diagrams). Two books rather more readable and stimulating than most are the latest editions of J. A. Kay, *The British Tax System* (Oxford University Press), and S. James and C. Nobes, *The Economics of Taxation* (Prentice Hall).

AUDIT

The main function of the auditors of a company is to report to the shareholders whether in their opinion the financial statements give a true and fair view. A good introductory book is T. A. Lee, *Corporate Audit Theory* (International Thomson, 1993). The text of auditing standards and guidelines is set out in the latest edition of *Auditing and Reporting* (Institute of Chartered Accountants in England and Wales). For further information see the latest edition of P. Chidgey and J. Mitchell, *Implementing GAAS* (Accountancy Books). A discussion of how auditing can be improved can be found in W. M. McInnes, ed., *Auditing into the Twenty-first Century* (Institute of Chartered Accountants of Scotland, 1993).

ACCOUNTING REGULATION AND ACCOUNTING CONCEPTS

Regulation, formats, accounting standards, conceptual frameworks, foreign exchange, and creative accounting were discussed in Chapter 4.

In Britain, decisions about disclosure, presentation and valuation are mainly in the hands of the government, through company law, and the accountants, through accounting standards issued by the Accounting Standards Board.

Financial statements are based mainly on historical costs modified by prudence and by the revaluation of some fixed assets.

As noted in Chapter 5, all extant accounting standards and exposure drafts are reproduced in *Accounting Standards*, revised annually and published by the Institute of Chartered Accountants in England and Wales. A good book on measurement problems is G. Whittington, *Inflation Accounting: An Introduction to the Debate* (Cambridge University Press, 1983). A number of classic articles are brought together in R. H. Parker, G. C. Harcourt and G. Whittington, eds, *Readings in the Concept and Measurement of Income* (Philip Allan, 2nd edn, 1986).

TOOLS OF ANALYSIS

Chapter 5 was concerned with defining and explaining the uses and limitations of ratios, percentages and yields as tools for the analysis of financial statements. George Foster, *Financial Statement Analysis* (Prentice-Hall, 2nd edn, 1986) and B. Rees, *Financial Analysis* (Prentice-Hall, 2nd edn, 1995) are very thorough treatments of the subject. There are relevant chapters in John Sizer, *An Insight into Management Accounting* (Penguin, 3rd edn, 1989).

PROFITABILITY, RETURN ON INVESTMENT AND VALUE ADDED

Profitability, return on investment and value added were discussed in Chapter 6, in which the relationships between sales, profits and assets were considered.

LIQUIDITY AND CASH FLOWS

In Chapter 7 it was pointed out that a company must be liquid as well as profitable and that making profits is not the same as accumulating cash. It was shown that the best way to control liquidity from inside the company is by means of a cash budget.

The external analyst uses the current ratio and the liquid ratio as rather cruder measures. Other indicators of liquidity are the defensive interval, the average collection period and stock turnover. The extreme case of illiquidity is insolvency; some success has been achieved in predicting this by means of financial ratios.

SOURCES OF FUNDS AND CAPITAL STRUCTURE

Chapter 8 discussed sources of funds and capital structure. It was pointed out that shareholders are still the most important source of long-term funds, especially through the medium of retained profits, but that loans and other borrowings are also of importance.

The problem of capital structure is to obtain the best mix of debt and equity. Factors to be considered are cost, risk, control, acceptability and transferability. It was argued that either the earnings yield (reciprocal of the price–earnings ratio) or the dividend yield plus a growth rate are better measures of the cost of equity than the dividend yield itself. The imputation system of corporate taxation and the possibility of dilution complicate the calculation of measures of earnings per share.

Risk can be approached through traditional measures of gearing or through the calculation of betas, which quantify the market risk of a share as distinguished from its specific risk.

In deciding on its dividend policy, a company looks at its effect on the cost of capital, on dividend yield and on dividend cover, and has to take account of government policy, inflation and taxation. Most companies try to pay a constant or moderately increased dividend (in money terms) each year, ironing out fluctuations in earnings.

Rights issues give existing shareholders the first chance to subscribe to new issues. They are distinguished from bonus issues, where the existing shareholders receive extra shares without further subscription.

After explanations of convertible loan stock, options, warrants and leasing, the chapter ended with a brief discussion of off balance sheet financing.

There are a number of good books on the topics discussed in Chapters 6, 7 and 8. Readers of the financial press should consult R. Vaitlingam, *The Financial Times Guide to Using the Financial Pages* (Financial Times/ Pitman Publishing, 1996). Two well-established textbooks are J. M. Samuels, F. M. Wilkes and R. E. Brayshaw, *Management of Company Finance* (International Thomson, 6th edn, 1995), and R. A. Brealey and S. Myers, *Principles of Corporate Finance* (McGraw-Hill, 5th edn, 1996).

PERSONAL INVESTMENT

This book has not dealt, except incidentally, with problems of personal investment. Its primary purpose has been to explain and interpret company annual reports and financial statements, not to advise the reader directly on how to invest his or her money on the stock market. It is not perhaps out of place, however, to conclude by recommending a book which does do this: J. Rutterford, *Introduction to Stock Exchange Investment* (Macmillan Press, 2nd edn, 1993).

Appendix A
Debits and Credits (Double Entry)

Welche Vorteile gewährt die doppelte Buchhaltung dem Kaufmanne!

Johann Wolfgang von Goethe, *Wilhelm Meisters Lehrjahre*, I, x

Most people know that accountants are concerned with debits and credits. Since it is possible to learn quite a lot about accounting and finance without using these terms, it has not been thought necessary to explain their meaning within the body of this book. Very little extra effort is required, however, to understand the underlying principles of double entry, so a brief explanation is given in this appendix.

It will be remembered from Chapter 2 that

assets = liabilities + shareholders' funds.

An increase on the left-hand side of this equation is called a debit (abbreviated to Dr.), an increase on the right-hand side a credit (abbreviated to Cr.). Similarly, decreases on the left-hand side are credits, and decreases on the right-hand side are debits. Debit and credit are used here as technical terms and should not be confused with any other meanings of these words.

It will also be remembered that shareholders' funds can be increased by the retention of profits and that retained profits is equal to revenues less expenses, tax and dividends. Since increases in retained profits are credits, it follows that increases in revenues are also credits, whereas increases in expenses, taxes and dividends must be debits. Conversely, decreases in revenues are debits and decreases in expenses, taxes and dividends are credits.

We can sum up the rules as follows:

DEBITS ARE		CREDITS ARE	
Increases in:	assets expenses taxes dividends	Increases in:	liabilities share capital revenues
Decreases in:	liabilities share capital revenues	Decreases in:	assets expenses taxes dividends

It seems curious at first sight that both increases in assets and in expenses are debits. In fact, assets and expenses are much more closely linked than is usually realized. If a company buys for cash a machine which is expected to last ten years, it is rightly regarded as having acquired the asset machine (increase in machines, therefore debit 'machines') in exchange for the asset cash (decrease in cash, therefore credit 'cash'). Suppose, however, that technological change is so rapid that these machines have an economic life of only one year or less. Then, if the accounting period is one year, the machine can be regarded as an expense of the period (therefore, debit 'machine expense', credit 'cash'). Thus, in one sense, an asset is merely an expense paid for in advance which needs to be spread over several accounting periods in the form of depreciation.

The system of debits and credits is referred to as double entry, since maintenance of the accounting equation requires that any increase or decrease in one item be balanced by a corresponding increase or decrease in another item or items. There are always two sides to any transaction. Suppose, for example, that a company decreases its cash by £100. The other side of the transaction might be:

1. An increase in another asset such as a machine (so, debit 'machine', credit 'cash').
2. A decrease in a liability, such as a trade creditor (so, debit 'creditor', credit 'cash').
3. An increase in a negative shareholders' funds item such as expenses, taxes or dividends (so, debit 'expenses', 'taxes' or 'dividends', credit 'cash').

Note that cash is always credited (since the asset cash has been decreased) and that a negative credit is the same as a debit (and a negative debit the same as a credit).

Appendix B

Glossary of Accounting and Financial Terms

This glossary serves two purposes:

1. To collect in alphabetical order various definitions, descriptions and explanations scattered throughout the text.
2. To provide certain *additional* information, especially concerning those matters which must by law be disclosed in the published financial statements of companies.

For more detail see R. H. Parker, *Macmillan Dictionary of Accounting* (Macmillan Press, 2nd edn, 1992).

Abbreviated accounts. Financial statements in which advantage has been taken of the exemptions available to SMALL COMPANIES and MEDIUM COMPANIES.

Accelerated depreciation. The writing off of depreciation (e.g., for tax purposes) at a faster rate than is justified by the rate of use of the asset concerned.

Accounting concepts. The assumptions which underlie periodic financial statements. Examples explained in this glossary are ACCRUALS, CONSISTENCY, GOING CONCERN, MATERIALITY, OBJECTIVITY, PRUDENCE and SUBSTANCE OVER FORM.

Accounting identity (or equation). Another name for the BALANCE SHEET IDENTITY.

Accounting period. The period between two balance sheets, usually a year from the point of view of shareholders and taxation authorities. Corporation tax is assessed on the basis of a company's accounting period.

Accounting policies. The accounting methods selected and consistently followed by a business enterprise. Companies publish a list of accounting policies in their annual reports.

Accounting reference period. A company's accounting period as notified to the REGISTRAR OF COMPANIES.

Accounting standards. See FINANCIAL REPORTING STANDARDS; STATEMENTS OF STANDARD ACCOUNTING PRACTICE.

Accounting Standards Board (ASB). The body prescribed in the UK under company law as a standard setting body. It issues FINANCIAL REPORTING STANDARDS and has endorsed the STATEMENTS OF STANDARD ACCOUNTING PRACTICE issued by its predecessor, the ACCOUNTING STANDARDS COMMITTEE.

Accounting Standards Committee (ASC). A committee established by the major professional accountancy bodies in the UK and Ireland which, from 1970 to 1990, prepared STATEMENTS OF STANDARD ACCOUNTING PRACTICE.

Accounts payable. Amounts owing by a company; usually called creditors in Britain.

Accounts receivable. Amounts owing to a company; usually called debtors in Britain.

Accruals. The accounting concept that revenues and expenses are recognized as they are earned or incurred, not as money is received or paid (accruals basis of accounting as distinct from cash basis).

Accumulated depreciation. The cumulative amount of depreciation written off a fixed asset at a balance sheet date.

Acid test. Another name for the LIQUID RATIO.

Acquisition accounting. A system of accounting which assumes the acquisition of one company by another rather than their merger. Compare MERGER ACCOUNTING.

Aktiengesellschaft (AG). The approximate German equivalent of the British PUBLIC LIMITED COMPANY.

Allotment. The allocation of shares by the directors of a company following applications for them by intending shareholders.

Alternative accounting rules. The rules set out in the Companies Act allowing the application to company financial statements of accounting valuations based on a variety of methods other than historical cost.

Amortization. The writing off over a period of an asset (especially an

INTANGIBLE FIXED ASSET) or a liability. Sometimes used synonymously with DEPRECIATION.

Annual general meeting (AGM). Meeting of the members (shareholders) of a company held annually at intervals of not more than fifteen months (but the first AGM may be held within eighteen months of formation). Usual business transacted: reception of directors' report and accounts; declaration of dividend; election of directors; appointment of auditors.

Annual report. Report made annually by the directors of a company to its shareholders. Its contents are largely determined by company law and accounting standards.

Annual return. Document which must be completed within forty-two days of the ANNUAL GENERAL MEETING and forwarded forthwith to the REGISTRAR OF COMPANIES. Main contents are:

(1) address of registered office;
(2) addresses where registers of members and debenture-holders are kept;
(3) summary of share capital and debentures, giving number of issued shares of each class, the consideration for them, details of shares not fully paid-up, etc;
(4) particulars of mortgages and charges;
(5) list of names and addresses of past and present shareholders giving number of shares held and particulars of transfers;
(6) names, addresses and occupations of directors and secretaries (and nationality of directors).

Copies of the financial statements, directors' report and auditors' report must be annexed to the return.

All the above can be inspected at the Companies Registries in Cardiff or Edinburgh on payment of a fee.

Applicable accounting standards. ACCOUNTING STANDARDS issued by a prescribed standard setting body (currently the ACCOUNTING STANDARDS BOARD). Companies other than small and medium-sized companies must state whether their accounts have been prepared in accordance with such standards and give particulars of any material departure therefrom and the reasons therefor.

Application money. The amount per share or unit of stock payable on application for a new issue of shares or debentures.

Articles of association. The internal regulations of a company. They usually deal with: rights of various classes of shares; calls on shares; transfer, transmission and forfeiture of shares; alteration of share capital; general meetings (notice, proceedings); votes and proxies; directors (powers, duties, disqualification, rotation, proceedings); dividends and reserves; accounts; capitalization of profits; audit; winding up; and similar matters.

Assets. Rights or other access to future economic benefits controlled by a company as a result of past transactions or other events. Examples include machinery, stock-in-trade, debtors, cash, goodwill.

Associated undertaking. An undertaking other than a subsidiary in which an investing group has a PARTICIPATING INTEREST and exercises significant influence.

Audit committee. A committee appointed by a company as a liaison between the board of directors and the AUDITORS. Audit committees normally have a majority of NON-EXECUTIVE DIRECTORS.

Audit expectations gap. The gap between what users expect from AUDITORS and what they think they are currently receiving.

Auditing Practices Board. The body responsible for the issue of AUDITING STANDARDS and auditing guidelines. Half of its members are practising auditors and half non-practitioners.

Auditing standards. Standards issued by the AUDITING PRACTICES BOARD designed to give credibility to the independence, objectivity and technical skill of AUDITORS.

Auditors. Independent experts who report to the shareholders of a company their opinion on the truth and fairness of published financial statements. Their remuneration (including expenses) must be disclosed. A person is eligible for appointment as the auditor of a company only if he or she is a registered auditor and is a member of a recognized supervisory body (e.g., one of the three institutes of chartered accountants) and is eligible for appointment under the rules of that body. The auditor must not be an officer or servant of the company or of a company in the group; a body corporate; or a partner or employee of an officer or servant of the company or a company in the group.

Authorized share capital. The maximum share capital which the directors of a company can issue at any given time. Disclosed in the balance sheet or the notes.

Average collection period. The average speed at which a company collects its debts:

$$\frac{\text{debtors} \times 365}{\text{credit sales}} \text{ days.}$$

Bad debt. An amount owing which is not expected to be received. It is written off either directly to profit and loss account or by way of a previously established provision for bad (or doubtful) debts.

Balance sheet. Statement of the assets, liabilities and shareholders' funds of a company at a particular date. The Companies Act prescribes a choice of two balance sheet formats and requires that every balance sheet shall give a true and fair view of the state of affairs of the company.

Balance sheet identity (or equation). The identity: assets *equals* liabilities *plus* shareholders' funds.

Bearer securities. Debentures or shares which are not registered and are transferable by simple delivery.

Beta. A measure of the market (or systematic) risk of a company's shares (i.e., the sensitivity of the share price to movements in the market).

Big five. The five largest public accountancy firms worldwide.

Bonds. Fixed interest securities such as government or company loans.

Bonus shares. Shares issued to existing shareholders without further payment on their part. Also referred to as a scrip issue, a capitalization issue and (in the USA) a stock dividend.

Book value. The monetary amount of an asset as stated in the balance sheet and books of account.

Brands. A means of distinguishing a product (and sometimes its manufacturer or distributor) from its competitors. An example of an INTANGIBLE FIXED ASSET.

Called-up share capital. The amount of the ISSUED SHARE CAPITAL which has been called up (i.e., the amounts shareholders have been asked to pay to date). Equal to the paid-up share capital unless there are calls in arrears or calls have been paid in advance.

Calls. Demands by a company for part or all of the balance owed on partly paid shares.

Capital allowance. In effect, the depreciation allowable for tax purposes. At times it has differed quite substantially from that charged in the published financial statements.

Capital employed. Usually refers to the total of shareholders' funds plus long-term debt, but may be used to refer to FIXED ASSETS plus NET CURRENT ASSETS.

Capital expenditure. Expenditure on FIXED ASSETS. The amount of contracts for capital expenditure not provided for and the amount of capital expenditure authorized by the directors but not contracted for must be disclosed.

Capital gain. A gain resulting not from operations but from the holding of an asset.

Capital gains tax. A tax on individuals. Companies pay CORPORATION TAX on their capital gains, not capital gains tax.

Capitalization issue. *See* BONUS SHARES.

Capitalize. To recognize as an asset.

Capital redemption reserve. When shares are redeemed otherwise than out of a new issue of shares, a sum equal to their nominal value must be transferred to an account with this name. For most purposes this reserve is treated as if it were SHARE CAPITAL.

Capital structure. The composition of a company's sources of funds, especially long-term.

Cash budget. A plan of future cash receipts and payments based on specified assumptions concerning sales growth, credit terms, etc.

Cash flow. The flow of cash into and out of a company. Often used loosely to refer to net profit plus depreciation, which is the result of movements in WORKING CAPITAL rather than cash.

Cash flow statement. A statement showing a company's inflows and outflows of cash during an accounting period. Can be prepared by the 'direct method' or the 'indirect method'. Cash flows are classified under the following headings: operating activities, returns on investments and servicing of finance, taxation, capital expenditure and financial investments, acquisitions and disposals, equity dividends paid, management of liquid resources, financing.

Chairman's review (or statement). Statement made by the chairman of a company at its annual general meeting and often included in the annual report. There are no legal regulations relating to its contents, but it often contains interesting and useful information.

Close company. A company resident in the UK which is under the control of five or fewer participators, or of participators who are directors. Introduced by the Finance Act 1965.

Combined Code. A voluntary code on CORPORATE GOVERNANCE that is backed up by a Stock Exchange listing requirement.

Common stock. American term for ORDINARY SHARES.

Company. Rather imprecise term implying corporate activity. This book deals with companies registered under the Companies Act. The liability of such companies is limited (either by shares or by guarantee), except in the case of unlimited companies.

Comparability. An accounting concept which emphasizes ease of comparison of the financial statements of different companies at a point in time.

Conservatism. *See* PRUDENCE.

Consistency. An accounting concept which emphasizes consistency of ACCOUNTING POLICIES over time for a particular company rather than COMPARABILITY of the financial statements of different companies at any one point in time.

Consolidated balance sheet. Balance sheet of a group of companies as distinct from the parent company only.

Consolidated profit and loss account. Profit and loss account of a group of undertakings as distinct from the parent company only. A parent company need not publish its own profit and loss account as well if the consolidated profit and loss account discloses the requisite details (*see* PROFIT AND LOSS ACCOUNT) and also discloses what portion of the consolidated profit (or loss) has been dealt with in its accounts.

Consolidation of share capital. Combination of shares into larger units (e.g., combining two 50 p shares into one of £1).

Contingencies. Conditions which exist at the balance sheet date the outcome of which will be confirmed only on the occurrence or non-occurrence of one or more uncertain events. Contingent liabilities must be disclosed as a note to the balance sheet.

Convertible loan stock. Loan stock which may be converted at the option of the holder at a future date or dates into ordinary stock at given price ratios.

Copyright. A right to published material. An INTANGIBLE FIXED ASSET.

Corporate governance. The processes by which companies are governed, including the relationships between shareholders, directors (executive and non-executive), third parties (e.g., creditors) and auditors, and the regulation of companies by the state.

Corporation tax. A tax on the profits of companies; not payable by individuals. The rate may vary. There is a lower rate for small profits.

Cost of capital. The cost to a company of obtaining funds for investment.

Cost of sales. The cost of goods sold during a period, calculated by adjusting cost of goods purchased or manufactured by the change in stocks. Also known as cost of goods sold.

Cost of sales adjustment (COSA). An adjustment made in CURRENT COST ACCOUNTING in order to base the cost of goods sold on the cost current at the time of consumption instead of the time of purchase.

Coupon rate of interest. The rate of interest on the par value of a debenture or bond. Not necessarily equal to the EFFECTIVE RATE.

Creative accounting. The use of accounting to mislead rather than help the intended user. *See also* OFF BALANCE SHEET FINANCING; WINDOW-DRESSING.

Credit. *See* DOUBLE ENTRY.

Creditors. Amounts, representing either cash or a claim to services, owed to a company. A distinction is made between amounts falling due within one year (also known as CURRENT LIABILITIES) and amounts falling due after more than one year.

Cum. Latin for 'with'. A price so quoted includes any dividend (div.), bonus issue, rights or other distribution.

Cumulative preference shares. PREFERENCE SHARES entitled to be paid the arrears of their dividend before any dividend is paid on the ordinary shares. Any arrears must be disclosed in the notes.

Current assets. Those ASSETS that are not intended for continuing use in a company's business; for example, cash, debtors and stocks. If the directors believe that any of the current assets will not realize their balance sheet values in the ordinary course of business, this fact must be disclosed. The alternative terms 'circulating assets' and 'floating assets' are obsolete.

Current cost accounting. A system of accounting in which assets are stated at the VALUE TO THE BUSINESS and current costs instead of historical costs are matched against revenues.

Current liabilities. LIABILITIES which are expected to have been paid within one year from the date of the balance sheet (e.g., trade creditors, proposed final dividend, current taxation).

Current purchasing power (CPP) accounting. A system of accounting which adjusts historical cost accounts for changes in the general price level.

Current ratio. Ratio of current assets to current liabilities. A measure of liquidity.

Current taxation. Tax payable within one year from the date of the balance sheet.

Debenture discount. Arises from issuing debentures at less than their par value. Disclosed in balance sheet to the extent that it is not written off.

Debentures. Loans, usually, but not necessarily, secured on the assets of the company. Usually redeemable but may be irredeemable.

Debit. *See* DOUBLE ENTRY.

Debtors. Amounts owing to a company. They are classified for disclosure purposes into the following categories:
(1) trade debtors;
(2) amounts owed by group undertakings;
(3) amounts owed by associated undertakings;
(4) other debtors;
(5) called-up share capital not paid;
(6) prepayments and accrued income.
Any amounts which fall due after more than one year must be shown separately for each category.

Defensive interval. A measure of how many days' operating expenses can be paid out of liquid assets.

Deferred taxation. Taxation arising from timing differences between accounting profit and taxable income. The potential amount of deferred taxation payable is disclosed in the notes. Only deferred taxation which is reasonably likely to have to be paid within the foreseeable future is included in the balance sheet in the UK.

Depreciation. A measure of the wearing out, consumption or other reduction in useful life of a FIXED ASSET arising from use, effluxion of time or obsolescence through technology and market changes. Amount of depreciation charged must be disclosed. Usually measured by allocating either the HISTORICAL COST or REPLACEMENT COST less SCRAP VALUE of the asset on a STRAIGHT-LINE or REDUCING-BALANCE basis. The accumulated (provision for) depreciation is deducted from the cost in the balance sheet to give the net book value. Depreciation is neither a source nor a use of funds.

Depreciation adjustment. An adjustment made in CURRENT COST

ACCOUNTING in order to base depreciation on current REPLACEMENT COST instead of HISTORICAL COST.

Deprival value. Synonym for VALUE TO THE BUSINESS.

Dilution. The decrease in control and/or earnings per share suffered by existing shareholders when a new issue of shares is wholly or partly subscribed to by new shareholders.

Directive. Within the European Union, a statement adopted by the Council of Ministers on the proposal of the European Commission. Directives are implemented through national legislation.

Directors' emoluments. The disclosure requirements are very detailed and complex. Emoluments can include salaries, fees, bonuses, expenses, allowances chargeable to UK income tax, the estimated money value of benefits in kind, pensions and retirement benefits, share options, and compensation for loss of office.

Directors' report. Annual report by the directors of a company to the shareholders. The directors of a non-small company must disclose in relation to a company and its subsidiaries:

(1) principal activities;

(2) an indication of the existence of branches of the company outside the UK;

(3) a fair review of the development of the business and any significant changes therein;

(4) an explanation of the relevance of the inclusion or exclusion of exceptional items in considering results or maintainable earnings;

(5) an indication of research and development activities;

(6) an indication of likely future developments;

(7) particulars of important events since the end of the year;

(8) proposed dividend of the company;

(9) any significant difference between the market value and book value of fixed asset interests in land;

(10) names of directors at any time during the year;

(11) interests in shares or debentures of group companies of each person who was a director of the company at the end of the financial year;

(12) where the company's average number of employees for the year exceeds 250, excluding employees working wholly or mainly outside the UK, the company's policy as to:

(a) employment of disabled persons, covering employment, training, career development and promotion

(b) employee involvement in company affairs, policy and performance;

(13) the separate totals of UK political and charitable contributions made during the year if together they exceed £200; and for individual political contributions exceeding £200, the amount and the identity of the recipient;

(14) the name of the director (or the secretary) who signed the report on behalf of the board;

(15) details of any company purchases of or interests in its own shares during the year;

(16) for public companies and their large subsidiaries, details of payment policy towards suppliers, and the number of days represented by trade creditors at the year end.

Listed companies are required by the Stock Exchange to disclose in addition:

(17) an explanation if results differ by 10 per cent or more from any published forecast or estimate;

(18) extra information regarding directors' interests and service contracts;

(19) substantial interests (i.e., normally 3 per cent or more) of any persons other than the directors in the share capital of the company;

(20) details of any significant contracts between the company or its subsidiaries and a controlling shareholder;

(21) a statement of whether the company has complied with the relevant paragraphs of the COMBINED CODE relating to corporate governance.

Discounted cash flow. The present value of future cash receipts and payments (i.e., their value after taking into account the expected delay in receiving or paying them).

Distributable reserves. A company's accumulated realized profits so far as not previously distributed or capitalized, *less* its accumulated realized losses so far as not previously written off in a reduction or reorganization of capital. Public companies may pay a dividend only if the net assets are not less than the aggregate of the called-up share capital and undistributable reserves.

Dividend. That part of the profits of a company which is distributed to the shareholders. May be interim (paid during the financial year) or final (recommended by the directors for approval by the shareholders at the annual general meeting). The proposed final dividend is shown in the balance sheet as a current liability.

Dividend cover. The ratio between EARNINGS PER SHARE and the ordinary dividend per share.

Dividend policy. A company's policy on how to divide its profits between distributions to shareholders (dividends) and reinvestment (retained profits).

Dividend yield. The relationship between the ordinary dividend and the market price per ordinary share, usually multiplied by an appropriate fraction to allow for the TAX CREDIT.

Double entry. A system of recording transactions based on the BALANCE SHEET IDENTITY. Broadly, increases in assets and decreases in liabilities and capital items (including expenses) are *debits*, and increases in liabilities and capital items (including revenues) and decreases in assets are *credits*.

Doubtful debt. Amount owing that a company is doubtful of receiving. It is usual to establish a provision for doubtful debts which is subtracted from gross DEBTORS (after deduction of BAD DEBTS).

Earnings per share (EPS). Net profit attributable to the ordinary shareholders (after tax and preference dividends) divided by the weighted average number of ordinary shares. May be calculated on a NET, NIL or MAXIMUM BASIS. The 'basic' EPS may be supplemented by a 'fully diluted' EPS to allow for share options and convertible loan stock. Companies often also report EPS based on earnings exclusive of exceptional items and discontinued operations.

Earnings yield. The relationship between the earnings per ordinary share and the market price per ordinary share. The reciprocal of the PRICE–EARNINGS RATIO multiplied by 100.

Effective rate of interest. The rate of interest on the market price of a debenture or bond. Not necessarily equal to the COUPON RATE OF INTEREST.

Employee information. The following must be disclosed:

(1) total average number of employees for the year and a division of this total by categories determined by the directors;

(2) staff costs divided into wages and salaries, social security costs, and other pension costs.

Employee report. A corporate financial report to employees, published either separately or as a supplement to a house magazine. Usually also made available to shareholders and other interested parties. May include a VALUE ADDED STATEMENT.

Equity method. Method of accounting for investments in associated undertakings. Sometimes called one-line consolidation.

Equity share capital. Defined by the Companies Act as any issued share capital which has unlimited rights to participate in either the distribution of dividends or capital. Often more narrowly defined to mean ORDINARY SHARES only.

Ex. Latin for 'without'. A price so quoted excludes any dividend (div.), bonus issue, rights or other distribution.

Exceptional items. Items exceptional on account of size and/or incidence which derive from the ordinary activities of a business and which need to be disclosed by virtue of their size or incidence. Compare EXTRAORDINARY ITEMS.

Executive director. A director of a company who is involved in its day-to-day operations.

Exposure draft. A draft FINANCIAL REPORTING STANDARD or STATEMENT OF STANDARD ACCOUNTING PRACTICE published for comment by interested parties.

Extraordinary items. Material items possessing a high degree of abnormality and which arise from events or transactions that fall outside the ordinary activities of the company and which are expected not to recur. Extremely rare in practice. Compare EXCEPTIONAL ITEMS.

Financial instrument. A document representing a promise to pay (e.g., a promissory note), an order to pay (e.g., a cheque) or a certificate of indebtedness (e.g., a DEBENTURE).

Financial ratio. Relationship among items in financial statements.

Financial reporting exposure draft (FRED). An EXPOSURE DRAFT issued by the ACCOUNTING STANDARDS BOARD.

Financial Reporting Review Panel. A review panel whose main task is to examine material departures by companies from company law and accounting standards. It has the power to apply to the court to enforce compliance with its findings.

Financial reporting standard for smaller entities (FRSSE). The only accounting standard that smaller entities (including small companies) are required to comply with. Provides a useful summary of accounting standards in many areas.

Financial reporting standards (FRSs). Standards issued by the ACCOUNTING STANDARDS BOARD.

Financial statements. Statements showing the financial position (balance sheet), gains and losses for a period (profit and loss account), and cash flows for a period (cash flow statement) of a company. A few companies also publish a VALUE ADDED STATEMENT.

Financial year. The most popular period for UK companies is 1 January to 31 December. For corporation tax purposes the year runs from 1 April to the following 31 March.

First year allowance. A CAPITAL ALLOWANCE granted in the first year of purchase of plant and machinery.

Fixed asset investments. Investments that are intended to be held for use on a continuing basis in the activities of a company.

Fixed assets. Those assets which are intended for use on a continuing basis in an undertaking's activities. Divided into INTANGIBLE FIXED ASSETS, TANGIBLE FIXED ASSETS and FIXED ASSET INVESTMENTS.

Fixed charge. A charge which is attached to some specific asset or assets.

Fixed overheads. Those overheads whose amount remains constant over the usual range of activity.

Flat yield. A YIELD which does not take account of the redemption value of a security.

Floating charge. A charge which is not attached to any specific asset but to all assets or to a class of assets.

Foreign currencies. The financial statements of foreign subsidiaries must be translated into sterling before they can be included in the consolidated statements. The method of translation, of which the most common is the 'closing rate method', must be disclosed. The parent company must also translate monetary assets it holds in foreign currencies.

Format. The method of presentation of a financial statement.

Gearing. The relationship between the funds provided to a company by its ordinary shareholders and the long-term sources of funds carrying a fixed-interest charge or dividend.

Gearing adjustment. An adjustment in current cost accounts intended to show the benefit to shareholders of the use of long-term debt, measured by the extent to which the net operating assets are financed by borrowing.

Gesellschaft mit beschränkter Haftung (GmbH). The approximate German equivalent of the British PRIVATE LIMITED COMPANY.

Going concern. An accounting concept which assumes that an enterprise will continue in operational existence for the foreseeable future.

Goodwill. The difference between the value of a company as a whole and the algebraic sum of the fair values of the assets and liabilities taken separately. Purchased non-consolidation goodwill is recorded when assets and liabilities are bought as a going concern from another enterprise. Such goodwill is treated in the same way as GOODWILL ON CONSOLIDATION.

Goodwill on consolidation. The excess of the cost of shares in subsidiary and associated undertakings over the fair value of their net tangible assets at the date of acquisition. Can only appear in a *consolidated* balance sheet.

Gross profit. The excess of sales over cost of sales.

Group accounts. Financial statements of a group of companies as distinct from those of the parent company only.

Guarantee, company limited by. A company the liability of whose members is limited to contributing a predetermined amount in the event of the company being wound up. Companies may be limited by guarantee or by shares, or be unlimited.

Harmonization. The process of narrowing differences in accounting practices, especially among countries.

Historical cost. The monetary amount for which an asset was originally purchased or produced. The traditional basis of valuation in published financial statements. Often modified in the UK by the revaluation of land and buildings. Favoured because it is more objective and more easily verifiable by an auditor.

Historical cost accounting rules. The rules set out in the Companies Act relating to the application to company financial statements of accounting valuations based on historical cost. Companies must follow either these rules or the ALTERNATIVE ACCOUNTING RULES.

Impairment. A reduction in the RECOVERABLE AMOUNT of a fixed asset (including goodwill) below the amount at which it is carried in the balance sheet.

Imputation system. System of corporate taxation under which all or part of the tax paid on distributed profits by the company is credited to the shareholders, thus mitigating double taxation.

Income statement. American term for PROFIT AND LOSS ACCOUNT.

Income tax. A tax on individuals; not payable by UK companies. Rates of income tax vary over time.

Industry ratio. An average ratio for an industry.

Inflation accounting. System of accounting which allows for changes in general and/or specific prices. *See also* CURRENT COST ACCOUNTING and CURRENT PURCHASING POWER ACCOUNTING.

Insolvency. An inability to pay debts as they fall due.

Institutional shareholders. Shareholders other than persons; industrial and commercial companies, the public sector and the overseas sector (especially financial institutions such as insurance companies and pension funds). Of increasing importance.

Intangible fixed assets. Non-monetary assets such as GOODWILL, PATENTS, TRADE MARKS, BRANDS and COPYRIGHTS which have no tangible form.

Interim dividend. *See* DIVIDEND.

Interim report. Report issued by a company to its shareholders during a financial year (e.g., quarterly, half-yearly).

Inventories. American term for stock-in-trade.

Investments. Shares, loans, bonds and debentures held either as fixed tangible assets or as current assets. Listed investments must be distinguished from unlisted.

Investment trust. Not really a trust but a company whose object is investment in the securities of other companies. Compare UNIT TRUST.

Irredeemable debenture. A DEBENTURE which will never have to be repaid.

Issued share capital. The amount of the AUTHORIZED SHARE CAPITAL which has been issued; the remainder is the unissued share capital. The amount of the issued capital must be disclosed in the notes. Not necessarily equal to called-up or paid-up share capital.

Issue expenses. Expenses of making an issue of shares or debentures. Disclosed in balance sheet to the extent that they are not written off.

Issue price. The price at which a share or debenture is issued; not necessarily equal to the PAR VALUE.

Joint venture. An entity, incorporated or unincorporated, which is jointly controlled by two or more other entities.

Leasing. Entering into a contract which allows the use of an asset in return for a periodic rental, but does not give ownership. In the case of long-term leasing, the effect is similar to financing the purchase of the asset by loan capital.

Leverage. The American term for GEARING.

Liabilities. The obligations of a company to transfer economic benefits as a result of past transactions or other events. Company law classifies them for disclosure purposes into the following categories:

(1) debenture loans;
(2) bank loans and overdrafts;
(3) payments received on account;
(4) trade creditors;
(5) bills of exchange payable;
(6) amounts owed to group undertakings;
(7) amounts owed to undertakings in which the company has a participating interest;
(8) taxation and social security;
(9) other creditors;
(10) accruals and deferred income;
(11) proposed dividends;
(12) convertible debt.

Listed companies are required by the Stock Exchange to show, subdivided between bank loans and overdrafts and other borrowings, the aggregate amounts repayable:

(1) in one year or less, or on demand;
(2) between one and two years;
(3) between two and five years;
(4) in five years or more.

All companies must distinguish between current and non-current liabilities.

Limited liability company. A company the liability of whose members is limited by shares or by guarantee. If by shares, liability is limited to the amount taken up or agreed to be taken up; if by guarantee, to the amount undertaken to be contributed in the event of winding-up.

Liquid assets. Current assets *less* stock-in-trade.

Liquid ratio. The relationship between liquid assets and current liabilities. Also known as the quick ratio, or the acid test.

Listed company. A public company listed (quoted) on a recognized stock exchange.

Listed investments. Investments which are listed on a recognized stock exchange or on any reputable stock exchange outside Great Britain. Must be shown separately in the balance sheet or notes thereto.

Loan capital. Funds acquired by non-short-term borrowing from sources other than the shareholders of the company.

Long-term debt. Long-term sources of funds other than equity (share capital and reserves).

Market capitalization. The total value on a stock exchange of a listed company's shares.

Market price. The price at which a company's securities can be bought or sold on a stock exchange. Not necessarily equal to the PAR VALUE or the ISSUE PRICE.

Materiality. An accounting concept that requires disclosure only of data that are significant enough to be relevant to the needs of a potential user.

Maximum basis. Method of calculating EARNINGS PER SHARE based on the assumption that a company distributes all its profits.

Medium companies. Companies with the privilege of filing abbreviated profit and loss accounts and notes with the REGISTRAR OF COMPANIES. 'Medium' is measured in terms of total assets, turnover and average number of employees.

Medium groups. *See* SMALL AND MEDIUM GROUPS.

Memorandum of association. A document which states:
(1) the name of the company;
(2) that the company is a public company (if such is the case);
(3) the situation of the registered office;
(4) the objects of the company;
(5) that the liability of the members is limited (unless the company is an unlimited one);
(6) the authorized share capital and how it is divided (or, in the case

of a company limited by guarantee, the maximum amount to be contributed by members on winding-up);

(7) details of the subscribers (the persons 'desirous of being formed into a company').

Merger accounting. A system of accounting which assumes the commercial substance of a merger of two or more companies rather than the acquisition of one by another. Compare ACQUISITION ACCOUNTING.

Minority interest. That part of a subsidiary company's shareholders' funds that is not held by the parent company. Usually shown as a separate item on the capital and liabilities side of a consolidated balance sheet.

Monetary assets. Assets (e.g., cash, debtors) which have a fixed monetary exchange value which is not affected by a change in the price level.

Monetary working capital adjustment (MWCA). An adjustment made in current cost accounting in order to take account of the effect of increased prices on monetary working capital (bank balances + debtors – creditors).

Net basis. Method of calculating EARNINGS PER SHARE which takes account of both constant and variable components in the tax charge.

Net current assets. Another name for WORKING CAPITAL.

Net profit. The excess of revenues over expenses. Calculated before or after extraordinary items and before or after tax, depending upon the context.

Net profit ratio. Ratio of net profit to sales.

Net realizable value. The amount for which an asset can be sold, net of the expenses of completion and of sale.

Net tangible assets. Assets other than INTANGIBLE ASSETS *less* LIABILITIES.

Net working capital. Another name for WORKING CAPITAL.

Nil basis. Method of calculating EARNINGS PER SHARE which assumes a nil distribution of dividends.

No credit interval. Another name for DEFENSIVE INTERVAL.

Nominal share capital. *See* AUTHORIZED SHARE CAPITAL.

Nominee shareholder. A shareholder who holds shares on behalf of another person or company who is the beneficial shareholder.

Non-executive directors. Directors who take no part in a company's day-to-day operations.

Non-monetary assets. Assets other than MONETARY ASSETS (e.g., tangible fixed assets and stock-in-trade).

Non-statutory accounts. Financial statements prepared for a purpose other than as part of a company's STATUTORY ACCOUNTS.

Non-voting shares. Shares with no voting rights. Non-voting ordinary shares are usually cheaper to buy than those which carry votes. Often called 'A' shares.

No par value shares. Shares with no nominal or par value. They are illegal in Britain.

Note of historical cost profits and losses. A calculation of what a company's profit on ordinary activities before taxation and retained profit would be if based entirely on historical cost accounting without, for example, any revaluation of fixed assets.

Notes to the accounts. Notes attached to and explanatory of items in the financial statements. May be very detailed.

Objectivity. Accounting concept which stresses the need to establish rules for recording financial transactions and events which so far as possible do not depend upon the personal judgement of the recorder.

Off balance sheet financing. Financing assets by 'borrowing' in such a fashion that the debt does not appear as a balance sheet item.

Operating and financial review. An analysis and explanation in an ANNUAL REPORT of the main features of a company's performance and financial position.

Operating profit. The excess of operating revenues over operating expenses, usually on an historical cost basis.

Ordinary shares. Shares entitled to share in the profits after payment of loan interest and preference dividends. Often referred to as the equity capital.

Overheads. Expenses other than the direct costs of material and labour.

Overtrading. A situation in which a company expands its sales and may appear to be highly profitable but does not have the resources available to finance the expansion and is therefore in danger of running out of cash.

Paid-up share capital. The amount of the CALLED-UP SHARE CAPITAL which has been paid up by the shareholders.

Parent undertaking. An undertaking that has one or more SUBSIDIARY UNDERTAKINGS. A parent undertaking of a group (other than a small or a medium group) must, if it is a company, prepare a CONSOLIDATED BALANCE SHEET and a CONSOLIDATED PROFIT AND LOSS ACCOUNT in addition to its own financial statements.

Participating interest. An interest in the shares of an undertaking which is held on a long-term basis for the purpose of securing a contribution to the investor by the exercise of control or influence arising from or related to that interest. A holding of 20 per cent or more is presumed to be a participating interest unless the contrary is shown.

Par value. The face or nominal value of a share or debenture. Not necessarily equal to the ISSUE PRICE or the current MARKET PRICE. Dividend and interest percentages refer to the par value, YIELDS to the current market price.

Patents. Grants by the Crown to the authors of new inventions giving them the sole and exclusive right to use, exercise and sell their inventions and to secure the profits arising therefrom for a limited period. An INTANGIBLE FIXED ASSET.

Post balance sheet events. Events occurring after the date of the balance sheet. They are either 'adjusting events' (those providing additional evidence of conditions existing at the balance sheet date) or 'non-adjusting events'.

Pre-acquisition profits. The accumulated profits of a subsidiary up to the date of its acquisition (takeover) by the parent.

Pre-emption right. The entitlement of an existing shareholder to an allotment of a proportionate part of a new issue of shares.

Preference shares. Shares which are usually entitled to a fixed rate of dividend before a dividend is paid on the ordinary shares and to priority of repayment if the company is wound up. Participating preference shares are also entitled to a further dividend if profits are available. If a preference dividend is not paid, the arrears must be disclosed in the notes. Arrears can only arise if the shares are *cumulative* as distinct from *non-cumulative*.

Preliminary announcement. An announcement, obligatory for listed companies, of the annual results of a company made by the directors before the full, audited accounts are published.

Preliminary expenses. Expenses of forming a company.

Price–earnings ratio. The multiple of the last reported EARNINGS PER SHARE that the market is willing to pay per ordinary share. The reciprocal of the EARNINGS YIELD multiplied by 100.

Prior charges. Claims on a company's assets and profits that rank ahead of ordinary share capital.

Priority percentages. Method of calculating GEARING by computing the percentage of earnings that is required to service each category of loan and share capital.

Prior year adjustments. Material adjustments applicable to prior years arising from changes in accounting policies or from the correction of fundamental errors.

Private limited company. A company which is not a PUBLIC LIMITED COMPANY. Not permitted to issue shares or debentures to the public. Its name must end in Limited or Ltd.

Profit. A general term for the excess of revenues over expenses. *See* GROSS PROFIT and NET PROFIT.

Profit and loss account. Statement of the revenue, expenses and profit of a company for a particular period. The Companies Act prescribes a choice of four profit and loss account formats and requires that every profit and loss account shall give a true and fair view of the profit or loss for the financial year. A published profit and loss account includes appropriations of profit and is therefore a combination of a profit and loss account proper and a PROFIT AND LOSS APPROPRIATION ACCOUNT.

Profit and loss appropriation account. Continuation of PROFIT AND LOSS ACCOUNT proper giving details of profit appropriations (i.e., distribution as dividends and retention as reserves).

Prospectus. Any notice, circular, advertisement or other invitation offering shares or debentures to the public.

Provision. Either a PROVISION FOR LIABILITIES AND CHARGES or a valuation adjustment; that is, an amount written off fixed assets (by way of depreciation or amortization) or current assets (e.g., a provision for doubtful debts). In both cases a charge is made to PROFIT AND LOSS ACCOUNT, but provisions for liabilities and charges are shown in the balance sheet as part of the liabilities, whereas valuation adjustments are deducted from the asset concerned.

Provision for liabilities and charges. Liabilities in respect of which the amount or timing of the expenditure that will be undertaken is uncertain. Examples include pensions and DEFERRED TAXATION.

Proxy. A person appointed to attend and vote at a company meeting on behalf of a shareholder, or the form, signed by the shareholder, which grants that authority.

Prudence. Accounting concept under which revenue and profits are not anticipated but are recognized by inclusion in the PROFIT AND LOSS ACCOUNT only when realized in cash or other assets, the ultimate realization of which can be assessed with reasonable certainty. Provision is made for all known liabilities, whether the amount of these is known with certainty or is a best estimate in the light of the information available.

Public limited company. A company whose MEMORANDUM OF ASSOCI-ATION states that it is a public company whose name ends with the words 'public limited company' (plc; ccc for Welsh companies) and which has a minimum authorized and allotted share capital, at least one quarter paid up, of £50,000. Unlike a PRIVATE LIMITED COMPANY, a public limited company is permitted to issue shares or debentures to the public.

Quasi subsidiaries. Companies which are legally not SUBSIDIARY UNDERTAKINGS of another company but are in fact controlled directly or indirectly by that company.

Quick assets. Current assets *less* stock-in-trade.

Quick ratio. *See* LIQUID RATIO.

Recognized supervisory body. An accountancy body recognized for the purpose of overseeing and maintaining the conduct and technical standards of company AUDITORS.

Reconciliation of movements in shareholders' funds. A note showing how the total of SHAREHOLDERS' FUNDS has changed during a financial year; for example, by the retention of profits and the issue of share capital.

Recoverable amount. The greater of the NET REALIZABLE VALUE of an asset and the amount recoverable from its further use.

Redeemable shares. Shares which must or may be redeemed at the option of the company or (very rarely) the shareholder. The balance sheet must disclose the earliest and latest dates on which the company has power to redeem, whether at the option of the company or in any event, and also the amount of any premium on redemption.

Redemption yield. A YIELD which takes into account not only the annual interest receivable but also the redemption value of a security.

Reducing-balance depreciation. Method of depreciation in which the periodic amount written off decreases over the life of the asset. A fixed percentage is applied to a declining written-down value.

Registered auditor. A person or firm whose name is inscribed on a statutory register as qualified for appointment as a company AUDI-TOR.

Registered office. The official address of a company. The MEMORANDUM OF ASSOCIATION must state whether it is in England, Wales or Scotland.

Registrar of Companies. Government officer with whom annual reports (including financial statements) and other documents must be filed; in Cardiff for companies registered in England and Wales, in Edinburgh for companies registered in Scotland.

Remuneration committee. A committee of non-executive directors of a listed company. Its report, published in the annual report, gives particulars of the company's policy on the remuneration of the executive directors. Details of the remuneration of individual directors is usually given in a note to the financial statements.

Replacement cost. The cost of replacing an asset.

Research and development expenditure. Includes expenditure on pure research, applied research and development. Only the last is in some circumstances treated as an asset.

Reserve. Reserves arise either from the retention of profits or from events such as the issue of shares at a premium or the revaluation of assets. Must not include PROVISIONS. Not a charge against profits and not usually represented by cash on the other side of the balance sheet. Movements in reserves during the financial year must be disclosed.

Reserve fund. A RESERVE which is represented by specially ear-marked cash or investments on the other side of the balance sheet.

Retained profits. Profits not distributed to shareholders but reinvested in the company. Their cost is less than a new issue of shares because of the issue costs of the latter.

Return on investment. Ratio of profit (usually before interest and tax) to NET TANGIBLE ASSETS. A measure of profitability.

Revaluation. The writing-up of an asset.

Revaluation reserve. The amount of gain or loss arising from the revaluation of any asset. An undistributable reserve unless the profit or loss has been realized.

Revenue expenditure. Expenditure that is written off completely in the PROFIT AND LOSS ACCOUNT in the accounting period in which it is made.

Reverse yield gap. A description of the fact that since August 1959 the average yield on government bonds has been greater than the average dividend yield on the ordinary shares of companies, despite the greater (monetary) security of the former.

Rights issue. An issue of shares in which the existing shareholders have a right to subscribe for the new shares at a stated price. The right can be sold if the shareholder does not wish to subscribe.

Risk. *See* SYSTEMATIC RISK and SPECIFIC RISK.

Sale and leaseback. Raising cash by selling an asset and then leasing it back in a long-term contract. *See also* LEASING.

Scrap value. The amount at which a FIXED ASSET is expected to be sold at the end of its estimated economic life.

Scrip issue. *See* BONUS SHARES.

Securities and Exchange Commission (SEC). American federal body concerned with the operations of corporations (i.e., companies) and issues of and dealings in their securities. It has the right, which it has largely allowed the Financial Accounting Standards Board to exercise, to establish accounting principles.

Security. Two meanings: (1) A generic name for stock, shares, debentures, etc.; (2) The backing for a loan.

Segmental reporting. Reporting the results of a diversified group of companies by major classes of business and geographical area. The Companies Act requires disclosure in the notes of turnover and profit or loss before taxation attributable to each class of business that, in the opinion of the directors, differs substantially from any other class. Turnover must also be disclosed by geographical markets where, in the opinion of the directors, these differ substantially from each other. ACCOUNTING STANDARDS extend these requirements for public companies, banking and insurance companies, and the larger private companies, requiring for both business and geographical segments the disclosure of turnover, profit or loss (before tax, minority interests and extraordinary items), and net assets.

Share capital. Unless limited by guarantee, a company registered under the Companies Act must have a share capital divided into shares of a fixed amount. The ownership of a share gives the shareholder a proportionate ownership of the company. The share capital is stated in the balance sheet at its par (nominal) value.

Shareholder. A member of a company the ownership of which is divided into shares.

Shareholders' funds. The proprietorship section of a company balance sheet. Includes the share capital and the reserves. Also known as shareholders' equity.

Share option. The right to buy or sell shares within a stated period.

Share premium. Results from issuing shares at a price higher than their par value. Must be disclosed in the balance sheet as a RESERVE. Cannot be used to pay dividends but can be used to make an issue of BONUS SHARES.

Simplified financial statements. Financial statements prepared so that those unskilled in accounting may more readily understand them. *See also* SUMMARY FINANCIAL STATEMENTS.

Small and medium groups. Groups of companies which are exempt from preparing and filing GROUP ACCOUNTS with the REGISTRAR OF COMPANIES. 'Small' and 'medium' are measured in terms of total assets, turnover and average number of employees.

Small companies. Companies with the privilege of filing an abbreviated balance sheet and notes and not preparing a profit and loss account and directors' report. 'Small' is measured in terms of total assets, turnover and average number of employees.

Small companies rate. A reduced rate of corporation tax paid by companies with small taxable incomes. This tax relief is not related to small companies as defined in the Companies Act.

Société anonyme (SA). The approximate French equivalent of a British PUBLIC LIMITED COMPANY.

Société à responsabilité limitée (SARL). The approximate French equivalent of a British PRIVATE LIMITED COMPANY.

Solvency. The ability of a debtor to pay debts as they fall due.

Specific prices. The prices, observable in a market, of specific goods and services. The government provides specific price indices periodically in its publication *Price Index Numbers for Current Cost Accounting.*

Specific risk. Risk arising from factors specific to a company and not from the market generally.

Stakeholders. Persons with a stake in the operations of a company whether by ownership, financial interest or otherwise.

Statement of movements in reserves. A statement showing how each category of reserves (e.g., share premium, revaluation reserve) has changed during a financial year.

Statement of total recognized gains and losses. Statement bringing together those gains (e.g., profit for the year) and losses which have passed through the PROFIT AND LOSS ACCOUNT and those which have not (e.g., unrealized gain on revaluation of properties).

Statements of recommended practice (SORPs). Non-mandatory statements of accounting practice.

Statements of standard accounting practice (SSAPs). Statements of methods of accounting prepared by the former ACCOUNTING STANDARDS COMMITTEE and approved by the councils of the major professional accountancy bodies. Extant SSAPs have been adopted by the ACCOUNTING STANDARDS BOARD.

Statutory accounts. Financial statements prepared in accordance with the Companies Act for filing with the REGISTRAR OF COMPANIES.

Stock exchange. A market where shares, debentures, government securities, etc., are bought and sold.

Stocks and work in progress. Comprises goods or other assets purchased for resale; consumable stores; raw materials and components; products and services in intermediate stages of completion; and finished goods. Valued at the lower of cost (HISTORICAL COST under historical cost accounting, REPLACEMENT COST under current cost accounting) or NET REALIZABLE VALUE.

Stock turnover. Ratio of cost of sales (sometimes, sales) to stock-in-trade.

Straight-line depreciation. Method of depreciation in which the periodic depreciation charge is obtained by dividing the cost less estimated scrap value by its estimated economic life.

Subdivision of share capital. Splitting of shares into smaller units (e.g., splitting one £1 share into two shares each valued at 50 p).

Subsidiary undertaking. An undertaking that is controlled by a PARENT

UNDERTAKING. Its financial statements must be included in the GROUP ACCOUNTS unless the subsidiary is lawfully excluded from consolidation.

Substance over form. An accounting concept whereby transactions or other events are accounted for and presented in accordance with their economic substance rather than their legal form.

Summary financial statements. Financial statements permitted to be sent to the shareholders of listed companies summarizing the information contained in the annual accounts and directors' report. The latter need be sent only to shareholders who state that they wish to receive them. The form of the summary financial statements is prescribed by law.

Supplementary financial statements. Statements presented as additional to primary FINANCIAL STATEMENTS and explicitly or implicitly of less importance; for instance, historical cost statements can be supplemented by current cost statements.

Systematic (market) risk. Risk arising from the market, not from specific factors applicable to a company. Quantified as the BETA of a company's ORDINARY SHARES.

Table A. A model set of ARTICLES OF ASSOCIATION, which can be adopted by a company in full or in a modified form.

Take-over bid. An offer to purchase all, or a controlling percentage of, the share capital of a company.

Tangible fixed assets. Assets such as land and buildings, plant and machinery, and fixtures and fittings.

Taxable income. Income liable to tax. Not usually equal to the profit reported in a company's financial statements.

Tax credit. A credit received by shareholders at the same time as a dividend. Its amount is related to the rate of income tax. It can be set off against the liability to income tax on the gross dividend.

Times interest earned. The number of times that a company's interest payable is covered or earned by its profit before interest and tax.

Trade credit. Short-term source of funds resulting from credit granted by suppliers of goods bought.

Trade discount. A discount off the list price of a good. Sales and purchases are recorded net of trade discounts.

Trade mark. A distinctive identification, protected by law, of a manufactured product or of a service. An INTANGIBLE FIXED ASSET.

Trading on the equity. Using fixed-interest sources of capital to boost the return on the equity (ordinary shares).

True and fair view. The overriding reporting requirement for companies. The phrase is undefined but depends upon both the application of legal requirements and APPLICABLE ACCOUNTING STANDARDS and the exercise of judgement. If FINANCIAL STATEMENTS and the notes thereto do not in themselves give a true and fair view, additional information must be provided. In special circumstances the express requirements of the law and standards must be departed from if this is necessary in order to give a true and fair view. *A* true and fair view is required, not *the* true and fair view.

Turnover. Sales; that is, the amounts derived from the provision of goods and services falling within a company's ordinary activities after deduction of trade discounts, VAT and similar taxes. In consolidated financial statements it excludes inter-company transactions. *See also* SEGMENTAL REPORTING.

Ultra vires. Latin for 'beyond the powers'. Especially applied to acts of a company not authorized by the objects clause of its MEMORANDUM OF ASSOCIATION.

Undistributable reserves. The aggregate of: share premium account; capital redemption reserve; accumulated unrealized profits, so far as not previously capitalized, *less* accumulated, unrealized losses, so far as not previously written off in a reduction or reorganization of capital; and other reserves which a company is prohibited from distributing.

Unit trust. Undertaking formed to invest in securities (mainly ordinary shares) under the terms of the trust deed. Not a company. Compare INVESTMENT TRUST.

Unlimited company. A company the liability of whose members is limited neither by shares nor by guarantee.

Unlisted investments. Investments which are not listed on a recognized British stock exchange or on any reputable stock exchange outside Great Britain. If they consist of equity of other companies, directors must give either an estimate of their value or information about income received, profits, etc.

Unsecured loan. Money borrowed by a company without the giving of security.

Urgent Issues Task Force (UITF). A body which assists the ACCOUNTING

STANDARDS BOARD in areas where an accounting standard or legal requirement exists, but where unsatisfactory or conflicting interpretations have developed or seem likely to develop. The UITF seeks to reach a consensus to which companies are expected to conform.

Value added statement. A statement showing for a period the wealth created (value added) by the operations of an enterprise and how the wealth has been distributed among employees, government, providers of capital, and replacement and expansion.

Value added tax (VAT). A tax based on the value added as goods pass from supplier of raw materials, to manufacturer, to wholesaler, to retailer, to consumer. Tax receivable can be set off against tax payable. Turnover is shown net of VAT in published profit and loss accounts.

Value to the business. The deprival value of an asset; that is, the lower of its current replacement cost and RECOVERABLE AMOUNT. The basis of valuation in current cost accounting.

Variable overheads. Overheads which vary proportionately with manufacturing activity.

Warrants. Certificates giving the holder the right to purchase a security at a predetermined price at a future date or dates.

Window-dressing. The manipulation of figures in financial statements so as to produce a desired appearance and ratios on the balance sheet date.

Working capital. Current assets *less* current liabilities.

Work-in-progress. Partly completed manufactured goods.

Writing-down allowance. The annual amount deductible for tax purposes on certain TANGIBLE FIXED ASSETS.

Written-down value. The value of an asset in the books of a company or for tax purposes after depreciation or capital allowances have been written off.

Yield. The rate of return relating cash invested to cash received (or expected to be received).

Z-score. A measure of the SOLVENCY of a company calculated from an equation incorporating more than one FINANCIAL RATIO.

Appendix C

Annual Report and Accounts of British Vita PLC
for the Year Ended 31 December 1997

Please note that this appendix closely reproduces the British Vita PLC report and accounts for 1997, and that the original pagination has been retained. A blank page indicates a page of photographs in the original report and accounts that has not been included here.

Contents

Vita is an International leader in the application of science, technology and engineering . . . to the production of specialised polymer, fibre and fabric components . . . for the furnishing, transportation, apparel, packaging and engineering industries throughout the world.

FINANCIAL HIGHLIGHTS

	1997	£m 1996
Turnover of continuing operations	808.4	873.5
Operating profit on continuing operations	55.5	49.9
Share of profits of continuing associated undertakings	9.6	8.3
Profit on ordinary activities before tax on continuing operations	66.2	58.4
Earnings per Ordinary share from continuing operations	19.8p	17.2p
Dividend per Ordinary share	8.75p	8.25p

Excellent progress

A most successful year in which we achieved record pre-tax profits of £66.2m, an improvement of 16% over the previous year, based upon volume growth of 5%.

Earnings per share on continuing operations have further improved by 15% to 19.8p and the dividend for the year is increased by 6% whilst at the same time maintaining our objective of building dividend cover.

Operating profits on continuing operations increased by 11% to £55.5m. The share of profits from our associates showed good progress, with Spartech again maintaining its strong growth and profit performance.

Our companies operate in many business climates which, overall, have proved to be more favourable in 1997. Our re-positioning in some of the tougher markets has enabled us to improve performance in those territories. Raw materials prices in the main remained stable throughout the year, with the exception of some reduction in polyester fibre prices and increases in specific polymers within the Industrial division. Generally, increases anticipated during the fourth quarter did not materialise.

Cash generation is again a strong feature of these results with continued acquisition activity and substantial capital expenditure.

Sterling's value against most other currencies remains high and whilst it has had minimal overall effect on profitability, it has impacted on the translation values of the sales of overseas subsidiaries and is responsible for more than the net decline in continuing sales.

Board changes

At the close of the forthcoming Annual General Meeting, Mr Duncan Lawton will retire from the Board after 30 years with Vita, 26 of those as a member of the Board. During this time, Duncan has made an outstanding contribution to the development of the Group and, on behalf of all shareholders, I wish him a long and happy retirement.

A suitable replacement for Mr Lawton as a non-executive director is actively being sought and I hope to announce an appointment in the near future.

Personnel

The continuing improvement in our performance is a challenge and testimony to the commitment, dedication and hard work of all employees and I would like to take this opportunity to thank everyone for their achievements.

The future

The start to the year has been encouraging in most areas of operation. The recent events in some of the Far Eastern and Asian economies suggest that raw materials prices should remain stable in the short to medium term. With regard to the turmoil in these economies, Vita is well positioned due to its geographic spread and product portfolio such that any effect is expected to be minimal.

We will continue, as ever, to maintain the unrelenting quest for competitiveness and to seek profitable growth by acquisition and investment to enhance further our position as a leading world player in the growing applications for polymer-based science technologies.

R. McGee CBE
9 March 1998

Improved margins and growth

I am pleased to report a strong 21% improvement in overall operating margin to 6.9% (5.7%), reflecting the considerable effort that has taken place at business level. In the second half of the year the margin increased to 7.3% from the 6.5% reported in the Interim results. Significantly, operating margins improved in all of the three main business sectors and principal geographic territories.

In the year the underlying sales volume increased by 4% and, more encouragingly, reached 7% in the second half of the year. The reported 7% net reduction in total sales was due, in the main, to the adverse translation effects on sales in overseas subsidiaries.

A high level of capital expenditure was maintained throughout the year amounting to £39m, most of which was targeted at organic growth and margin improvement programmes.

Acquisitions in the year were driven by the requirements identified from our strategic matrix. Within the Cellular group, Crest Foam Industries in the USA has extended our range of technical products for use in a broad spectrum of sophisticated industrial applications.

The joint venture in China and the recently announced investment in Brazil are further evidence of the commitment of Vita to the supply of automotive laminatable foams worldwide. Vita Baltic International, a foam manufacturing business, has been established in Lithuania to strengthen further our position in the fast growing East European comfort market.

In the Industrial division, the thermoplastic sheet businesses have been extended with the bolt-on acquisitions of Sopla (Italy) and Kunex (Germany) to reinforce our number one position in the European sheet market.

The acquisition of Silvergate Plastics in the UK will provide additional growth opportunities for our compounding division by opening up the new area of colour masterbatch production.

At the close of the year, the Fibres and Fabrics division completed the acquisition of Moulinage in France, substantially extending our speciality fibre processing business.

Health & Safety

The management of Health & Safety and Environmental procedures remains a priority. The Vita Health & Safety and Environmental policy calls for the commitment of all personnel to work together to improve Health & Safety in the workplace, strongly supported by the expertise of a central co-ordinating team working positively with the individual businesses.

Future opportunities

Vita, with its unique position as a world leader in each of its three distinct divisions, intrinsically linked by the common thread of polymer based technologies, is ideally placed to capitalise on the ever growing demand for polymer products. Our objective remains to strengthen further this position, seeking acquisitions and organic growth opportunities to achieve sustainable profit growth to maximise shareholder value.

J. Mercer Chief Executive
9 March 1998

Increased return on assets

Operating profit from continuing operations increased by £5.6m (11%) with earnings per share up 2.6p (15%). The return on shareholders' funds improved from 19% to 22%. Strong cash generation was achieved, with significant expenditure maintained on acquisitions and to fund organic growth.

Operating results

Sales from continuing operations decreased by £65m (7%) to £808m due to the further strengthening of sterling against other currencies during the year. The resulting adverse exchange rate translation movement on the sales of overseas subsidiaries amounted to £81m. Sales volume growth in the year was 5% including 1% from acquisitions.

Operating profit from continuing operations improved by £5.6m (11%) to £55.5m with acquisitions contributing £0.7m. Adverse exchange rate translation movements amounted to £4.4m although the impact of these was largely offset by lower raw material costs due to the appreciation of sterling.

The overall operating margin from continuing operations was significantly above the previous year at 6.9% (5.7%). Operating margins increased in all three geographic territories with the UK up to 8.5% (6.9%), Continental Europe to 5.7% (5.0%) and International to 5.0% (4.4%).

The increase in share of profits from associated undertakings reflects the continued strong performance at Spartech with 1997 reported earnings up 39%. Sales increased by 28% to $503m mainly due to the prior year acquisition of the Hamelin group.

Profit before taxation increased by £9m to £66.2m due primarily to the improved operating margins of the Group. The effective rate of taxation was in line with expectations at 33.5% (35%).

Earnings and dividends

Earnings per share on an FRS3 basis increased by 18% to 19.8p per share. The total dividend for the year is 8.75p per Ordinary share, an increase of 6% on 1996. The dividend is covered 2.3 times.

£m	1997	1996
Sales	£808.4m	£873.5m
Operating profit	£55.5m	£49.9m
Return on sales	6.9%	5.7%
Return on net assets	21%	19%

Cash flow

Expenditure on subsidiary undertakings and businesses acquired during the year totalled £19.9m (£34.9m), including net cash of £4.4m (net debt of £1.4m in 1996), and comprised:

	£m
Crest Foam Inc. – USA	5.7
Moulinage S.A. – France	5.8
Silvergate Plastics Ltd. – UK	5.4
Other acquisitions	3.0
	19.9

Goodwill arising on the acquisitions and associated investments of £23.1m has been dealt with through reserves.

Capital expenditure in the year amounted to £38.6m (£38m) and was 1.4 times depreciation (1.2 times). Sales of tangible assets realised £5.6m (£4.3m) and there was an outflow of £8.1m from working capital (inflow of £9.9m). Net cash flow for the year was an outflow of £10.3m (inflow of £6.8m).

Balance sheet

Shareholders' funds at 31 December 1997 were £286.1m, a decrease of £11.9m over the previous year. The movement comprises retained profits for the year of £24.4m and £1.2m of Ordinary shares issued on options exercised and PEP applications, less £23.1m goodwill dealt with through reserves and an adverse closing exchange rate balance sheet adjustment of £14.4m. The return on net assets improved to 21% with the return on shareholders' funds increasing from 19% to 22%.

Treasury operations

Treasury activities are co-ordinated by the Centre in accordance with policies and procedures as laid down in the Group accounting and internal control manual. Limits approved by the Board are in place covering counter parties, instruments, dealing and settlement. Treasury activities are subject to periodic internal and external audit.

Foreign exchange

The Group hedges net material foreign currency transaction exposures, arising from sale of goods and services overseas, purchase of raw materials and tangible fixed assets of foreign origin, through forward contracts.

When funds are required for businesses outside the UK, a combination of Sterling sourced funds (equity or shareholder's loans) and currency borrowing is used. Such borrowings provide a partial hedge against the effect of currency volatility on overseas assets and income. Targets are established for the proportion of net assets to be represented by currency debt. Funding decisions are taken in light of these targets but subject to local taxation and regulatory considerations.

Net cash and borrowings

The Group manages borrowing to ensure appropriate cost effective facilities whilst minimising risk. The current modest level of committed facilities reflects the historically strong balance sheet. Surplus cash assets are invested safely to maximise earnings within policies approved by the Board. Net cash at the year end reduced to £8m (3% of shareholders' funds) after a net cash outflow of £10.3m, finance leases acquired of £0.8m, share proceeds of £1.2m and an exchange rate translation gain of £1.6m.

Exchange rates

The principal exchange rates used in the preparation of the accounts are shown in the notes on page 28. Cumulative movements against major European currencies (Dm, Ffr, Dfl and Bfr) over the last two years now amount to nearly 30%.

Pension schemes

The detailed impact of the Government's announcement of the elimination of Advance Corporation Tax credits on dividends received by pension funds is currently under review. Work to date indicates that this will have a limited overall impact on the funds, and the Group, due to the conservative nature of the funding assumptions used. Full details on the treatment of pension costs are set out in note 10 on page 32.

C. J. O' Connor

C. J. O'Connor Finance Director
9 March 1998

SUMMARY OF FINANCIAL DATA 1993–1997

	1997	1996	1995	1994	£m 1993
Profit and Loss Account					
Turnover					
– continuing operations	808.4	873.5	817.8	716.0	682.0
– discontinued operations	–	22.3	57.8	53.0	72.2
Group turnover	808.4	895.8	875.6	769.0	754.2
Operating profit	55.5	49.9	45.8	47.3	41.4
Exceptional and discontinued operations	–	(0.9)	(14.0)	(2.3)	(7.9)
	55.5	49.0	31.8	45.0	33.5
Share of profits of associated undertakings					
– continuing operations	9.6	8.3	5.9	3.1	2.9
– discontinued operations	–	–	0.1	0.9	1.9
	65.1	57.3	37.8	49.0	38.3
Goodwill written off on discontinued operations	–	–	(3.3)	(0.8)	–
Closure, restructuring and disposal costs	–	(0.1)	(7.5)	–	(5.4)
Profit on disposal of associated undertakings	–	–	7.8	–	–
Profit on ordinary activities before interest	65.1	57.2	34.8	48.2	32.9
Net interest receivable	1.1	–	0.9	1.3	0.8
Profit on ordinary activities before taxation	66.2	57.2	35.7	49.5	33.7
Tax on profit on ordinary activities	(22.2)	(20.0)	(13.5)	(17.3)	(12.4)
Profit on ordinary activities after taxation	44.0	37.2	22.2	32.2	21.3
Minority interests	(0.2)	(0.3)	(0.3)	(0.2)	(0.7)
Profit for the financial year	43.8	36.9	21.9	32.0	20.6
Dividends	(19.4)	(18.2)	(17.5)	(16.8)	(15.9)
Retained profit for the year	24.4	18.7	4.4	15.2	4.7
Balance Sheet					
Tangible fixed assets	225.8	229.8	236.5	210.9	199.9
Investments	18.8	22.4	19.9	23.6	22.4
Net working capital	34.6	30.5	49.9	30.0	20.5
Net cash	8.0	16.3	4.6	30.2	38.1
Minority interests	(1.1)	(1.0)	(1.1)	(0.9)	(2.9)
Shareholders' funds	286.1	298.0	309.8	293.8	278.0
Ratios					
Operating profit as a percentage of Group turnover*	6.9%	5.7%	5.6%	6.6%	6.1%
Return on average shareholders' funds	22%	19%	12%	17%	12%
Return on average shareholders' funds normalised*	22%	19%	17%	18%	16%
Return on net assets	21%	18%	12%	20%	15%
Return on net assets normalised*	21%	19%	18%	21%	21%
Net cash	(3%)	(5%)	(2%)	(10%)	(14%)
Earnings per share	19.8p	16.8p	10.0p	14.7p	9.6p
Earnings per share normalised*	19.8p	17.2p	15.4p	15.1p	14.7p
Dividend per share	8.75p	8.25p	7.95p	7.7p	7.4p
Number of times covered	2.3	2.0	1.3	1.9	1.3
Net assets per share	129p	135p	141p	135p	129p
Average number of shares in issue	221.2m	220.2m	218.7m	216.6m	214.7m

* Excluding discontinued operations and exceptional items.

British Vita PLC   Annual Report & Accounts 1997

(150)

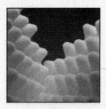

Cellular polymers

Vita sets the global standard for foam operations, utilising the very latest equipment, together with half a century of technical expertise.
Major product categories
Vita's urethane capabilities are extensive, in polyether block or moulded form, polyester in rolls, rebonded foam and a range of reticulated or impregnated foams. Vita also has significant involvement in polystyrene and latex foam manufacture.
Manufacturing locations
Worldwide manufacturing facilities spanning the UK, Continental Europe including expansion in Poland and Lithuania, the USA and Zimbabwe. Associated undertakings in Canada, Africa and recently in China.
Major markets
An extensive customer base, covering furniture and bedding, transportation, packaging, medical, electronics, footwear and apparel, carpet underlay, construction, engineering and a growing list of industrial applications.

Industrial

Vita is a leading player in the worldwide manufacture of engineering thermoplastic sheet and rollstock, specialist thermoset and thermoplastic polymer products, including compounds in both solid and liquid form.
Major product categories
ABS, Polystyrenes, Polyolefines and Polycarbonates, in sheets or rollstock. Specialist compounds range from elastomers to rigid and flexible PVC and also include the engineering strength of Nylon and the exciting

developments of thermoplastic elastomers including microcellular grades.
Manufacturing locations
A network of 50 thermoplastic sheet manufacturing lines across the UK and Continental Europe, with a major associated undertaking in the USA. Compounding in the UK, Continental Europe, Australia and New Zealand, with downstream expertise in the UK converting compounds into mouldings and extrusions.
Major markets
Vita's products, transformed by customers' forming, moulding or extrusion, benefit almost every industrial sector.

Fibres & fabrics

Vita is Europe's largest processor of polyester fibre. It is also the UK's only manufacturer of staple polyester fibre, with the ability to recycle reclaimed high grade PET waste.
Major product categories
Flame-retardant, weldable, hydrophobic and mouldable waddings, non-wovens, stitched fibrous webs and precision cut electrostatically treated fibre for the global flocking market.
An unparalleled range of texturised yarns and processed, continuous filament man-made fibre which complements warp knitting, coating and commission finishing services.
Manufacturing locations
Complex custom designed plant produces fibre in the UK, processed in the UK, Continental Europe and the USA. Yarn texturing in the UK and the most recent acquisition in Continental Europe.
Major markets
A wealth of applications in medical, hygiene and healthcare, upholstery and bedding, leisure and sportswear, lingerie and hosiery, automotive and general industrial, worldwide.

British Vita PLC   Annual Report & Accounts 1997

Sales	£459.7m
Operating profit	£32.1m
Return on sales	7.0%
Return on net assets	22%

Cellular polymers

The sector achieved significant improvement in profitability overall.

Production capability was increased with the acquisition of Crest Foam Industries Inc. in the USA and the purchase of assets to form Vita Baltic International based in Lithuania. An initial investment was also made in China, jointly with the Inoac Corporation of Japan.

Continued high levels of capital investment were maintained to improve the asset base including significant investment in a new foam production facility in eastern Poland to expand the operations of Vita Polymers Poland and to improve facilities in Lithuania.

The UK cellular polymer operations enjoyed a successful year. Vitafoam traded well in all divisions with additional facilities installed on several sites, including the mid-year relocation of the Ashton conversion site to a brand new factory. Ball & Young continued to expand the production of carpet underlay, particularly the Cloud 9 lightweight range. Kay-Metzeler also had a good year, developing the furniture moulding operation following the prior year sale of the automotive moulding business. The polystyrene operations had a particularly successful year.

Caligen traded well throughout the year and co-ordinated the efforts to expand Vita's capability as a worldwide supplier of laminatable foam, particularly for the automotive seating market. The recent establishment of Caligen Foam Brazil indicates further progress in fulfilling this objective.

In Continental Europe, demand levels generally remained more subdued but profitability was increased within the German operations by internal efficiency improvements.

The French operations performed well in the difficult local economy, with the automotive business continuing to improve.

In the Netherlands, good progress was made by the latex operations at Radium with the increased utilisation of their new capacity. The Draka and Caligen operations had a satisfactory year, with the transfer of the polyurethane foam production from Maastricht to the Draka site at Hillegom completed.

The new reticulation unit at Breda also came into full production in the year and Vita's involvement in this specialist market was substantially enhanced by the purchase of the similar facilities of Crest Foam Industries in the USA.

Elsewhere in the US, the operations of Vita Inc. had a difficult year in a very competitive market with flat automotive demand, though progress was made in improving internal efficiencies at most sites. Difficulties were encountered on one of the major conversion sites in coping with the logistics of a massive increase in volume from a substantial customer.

Vita Polymers in Poland had a successful year and work was virtually completed on a new production facility based at Lublin in eastern Poland. A new company was formed with local partners in Lithuania and work has started on the planned new production facility.

Internationally, a small joint venture investment was made in China and the Zimbabwe company had a successful year.

The associated undertakings in Nigeria, Canada and Eire all met or exceeded expectations.

Sales	£200.3m
Operating profit	£15.7m
Return on sales	7.8%
Return on net assets	23%

REVIEW OF OPERATIONS

Industrial

An overall improvement in profitability was achieved. Vita Thermoplastic Compounds expanded capacity in the UK with a move to a new factory and the acquisition of Silvergate Plastics provides new opportunities in colour masterbatch compounding. Thermoplastic sheet capacity was increased in France, Germany and Italy, the latter linked with relocation to a new, larger site.

The compounding businesses produced a good result, despite the adverse effects of the strong Sterling exchange rate in reducing export demand in the UK.

Vita Thermoplastic Compounds commissioned the new Middleton factory and expanded production capacity for thermoplastic elastomers.

The acquisition, in July, of Silvergate Plastics, based in Wrexham, created major new opportunities for Vita as a colour masterbatch producer.

The nylon compounder, Jackdaw in the UK and France, had a satisfactory year. Vita Liquid Polymers had a successful year, as did the similar RLA Polymers in Australia and New Zealand which continued to develop, having successfully integrated the prior year Roberts acquisition. Plans are at an advanced stage for the formation of a small joint venture in Malaysia.

Vitamol produced good results, following refocussing and investment in the rubber mouldings business. Vitacom also produced a satisfactory result.

The thermoplastic sheet businesses in the UK, Germany, Austria, France, Italy and Denmark achieved excellent growth. Capacity at the Metzeler Plastics site has been increased by the integration of the assets of Kunex acquired at the end of the year. The joint venture in Austria showed good improvement. Royalite Italy acquired certain of the sheet assets of Sopla and the total relocation of the facilities to a new site at Cuggiono, some 20 km from the existing Vittuone site, is well advanced with a major, new extruder already commissioned on this

site. The sheet business of Roon was integrated into the facilities at Gaillon and the small, residual, lighting business was sold during the year.

Spartech, the associated company in the USA, had another record year and continued to expand both organically and by acquisition, including the purchase in August of the assets of the Preferred Plastic Sheet division of Echlin Inc. In February 1998, Spartech announced agreement to purchase Polycom Huntsman Inc., a leading supplier of polymer compounds, colour and additive concentrates with an annual turnover of US$115m.

Sales	£148.4m
Operating profit	£7.7m
Return on sales	5.2%
Return on net assets	16%

Fibres and fabrics

A good performance was achieved by the fibre operations, particularly in the UK and USA. The year-end acquisition of Moulinage in France has expanded the specialist yarn texturising operations.

The UK fabrics results were adversely affected by site rationalisation problems.

Vitafibres in the UK enjoyed a very successful year, with good volume growth. The major expansion, at Pennine, of production of polyester fibre from waste sources was successfully commissioned in the year.

The operations of Libeltex in Continental Europe operated in a difficult climate and some rationalisation of production was undertaken in Germany. The French and Swedish operations had a satisfactory year. The success of the major new investment, primarily supplying the hygiene market, was maintained and approval has recently been given for another new fibre line on the main Belgian site.

In the USA, the fibre division of Vita Inc. had an excellent year and plans have recently been approved for a major increase of production capacity.

The yarn texturising operations of Mowbray performed well and plans were approved recently to extend further the Macclesfield site. Vita's interests in this specialised field were expanded by the acquisition at the very end of the year of Moulinage, based at Calais in France, giving the combined companies access to new markets and opportunities.

The Rossendale Combining laminating and finishing businesses produced an improved result.

The Vita-tex warp knitted textile business in the UK had a disappointing year, suffering from the inevitable disruption caused by the consolidation of the S.A.Driver business onto the Woodeaves site at Lancaster. The flocked fabric operation at Woodeaves was largely unaffected by the changes and achieved further market penetration.

DIRECTORS AND OFFICERS

Teamwork

R. McGee CBE, FIM, CIMgt, FRSA
Non-executive Chairman
Robert McGee, 63, joined Vita in 1955. He was appointed to the Board in 1972, became Chief Executive in 1975 and Chairman in 1988. He was awarded the CBE for services to industry in June 1994.

J. Mercer CEng, MIMfg E
Chief Executive
Jim Mercer, 52, with 27 years experience in Vita's UK elastomeric and automotive component operations, was appointed to the Board in October 1995, becoming Chief Executive in 1996.

F. J. Eaton FIM
Deputy Chief Executive
Frank Eaton, 58, joined Vita in 1958, was appointed to the Board in 1975 and became Deputy Chief Executive in 1991. He is currently President of the British Rubber Manufacturers Association.

K. R. Bhatt BCom, MCT, FRSA
Director
Kanak Bhatt, 58, joined Vita in 1966 and was appointed to the Board in 1991, serving as Finance Director until late 1996. Currently, as Chairman of the International Holding companies, he is involved in overseas development.

C. J. O'Connor BSc, FCA
Finance Director
Calvin O'Connor, 45, joined the Board in June 1996 and became Finance Director in November 1996.

F. J. Libeert BA, ATI
Director
Filiep Libeert, 44, who joined Vita in 1979, has Management Board responsibility for Netherlands cellular foam operations and Continental European fibre operations. He was appointed to the Board in October 1995.

L. D. Lawton OBE, DL, BA, FRSA
Non-executive Director
Duncan Lawton, 70, joined Vita in 1968, was appointed to the Board in 1972 and served as Deputy Chairman from 1988 to 1996. He was awarded the OBE in 1989 for services to industry.

M. A. Jones
Non-executive Director
Alan Jones, 62, was appointed to the Board in 1993 following retirement from a successful career with National Westminster Bank Group.

R. T. Scholes FCA
Non-executive Director
Richard Scholes, 52, was appointed to the Board in 1993. He is a director of Kleinwort Benson Securities Limited.

The executive directors also serve on the Management Board, on which they are joined by (from left above):
L. H. Butterworth, Chairman, UK, German and USA cellular polymers.
J. K. Smethurst, Chairman, UK fibres and fabrics and international cellular polymers.
R. Dobson, Chairman, international industrial operations.
P. Vassort, Chairman, cellular polymers in France.

Company Secretary: **A. R. Teague**, FCCA
Corporate Solicitor: **M. R. Stirzaker**, BA

DIRECTORS' REPORT

The directors have pleasure in presenting their annual report and accounts for the year ended 31 December 1997.

Profits and dividends

The profit for the financial year ended 31 December 1997 is £43.8m in the Group and £20.3m in the Company, before provision for dividends, paid and proposed, of £19.4m. Retained profit for the financial year of £24.4m has been transferred to reserves.

An interim dividend of 4.25p per Ordinary share was paid on 10 November 1997. The directors now propose a final dividend of 4.5p per Ordinary share payable on 11 May 1998 to shareholders on the Register at 20 March 1998, making a total Ordinary dividend for the year of 8.75p (8.25p) per share.

Principal activities

The principal operations of Vita are described on page 7, with the Group's principal subsidiary and associated undertakings listed on pages 43 and 44 of this report and accounts.

The principal operations, and changes thereto, are reviewed in the Financial Review on page 4 and the Review of Operations on pages 8 to 13, which form part of this Directors' Report.

Going concern

The directors report, in connection with paragraph 4.6 of the Cadbury Code, that after making enquiries they have a reasonable expectation that the Company has adequate resources to continue in operational existence. For this reason they continue to adopt the going concern basis in preparing the accounts.

Corporate governance

The directors acknowledge their responsibility for the operation of internal financial control systems with the objectives of safeguarding the Group's assets, maintaining proper and reliable accounting systems and therefore avoiding material mis-statement or loss.

However, such systems, including those operated within Vita summarised below, can only provide reasonable and not absolute assurance with respect to the preparation of financial information and the safeguarding of assets.

■ Vita is managed by a Main Board, consisting of the non-executive Chairman, five executive and three non-executive members, who retain responsibility for the formulation of corporate strategy, approval of acquisitions, divestments and major capital expenditure and treasury policy. Control of operational matters is delegated to a Management Board ensuring a strong link between strategy and implementation. Both Boards meet regularly to undertake their respective monitoring and co-ordinating functions. Current members of both Boards are listed on pages 14 and 15 of this report and accounts.

■ All non-executive directors constitute a Remuneration Committee, chaired by Mr McGee, to advise on both Board and senior staff remuneration policy, and they also form an Audit Committee, chaired by Mr Scholes, to review the half year and annual accounts and matters related to internal controls, including both the external audit and internal audit functions. When necessary, the entire Board constitutes a Nomination Committee.

■ Individual companies are managed by a local Board, chaired by a member of the Management Board, with a clearly defined responsibility for the operation of the business to meet standards required by both the Group and appropriate regulatory authorities. This includes the requirement for the production and submission to the Corporate Centre of regular accounts with commentary on current year performance as compared to planned performance, together with key ratio analysis and working capital information.

■ These accounts, prepared in accordance with Vita's accounting policies and principles, are consolidated and reviewed by the Management Board and, in summary, by the Main Board, to monitor overall performance and appropriate management intervention.

■ In addition, annual plans and longer term overviews of objectives are prepared by each business and reviewed with the local management team, at minuted meetings, by the appropriate Management Board member, supported by at least one executive director.

■ The Centre team monitors the funding requirements of, and the banking facilities provided to, individual operations, in addition to the management of investment and treasury procedures. Capital and significant investment expenditure is approved against pre-determined performance criteria through a tiered structure of authority limits from local to Main Board.

■ Individual business management is also responsible for assessing and minimising all business risks, supported by Centre personnel able to provide specific assistance in matters relating to health and safety, environment, quality systems and insurance cover for property and liability risks.

■ The internal audit function reviews systems in operation, together with appropriate compliance testing, to a programme pre-agreed with the Audit Committee and discussed with the external auditors. The procedures for internal audit are regularly reviewed to reflect the continuing development of internal systems and external best practice and work priorities are determined by agreement with the Management Board, taking into account the responses to a self-assessment questionnaire, completed by each business unit on an annual basis, on systems compliance.

The directors have reviewed the effectiveness of the systems operated throughout the year and will continue to do so, making any changes required as a result of the review and the natural development of the business.

Detailed reviews are also being undertaken on all sites, to assess the implications on Group systems of the year 2000.

In the opinion of the directors, Vita complies with the Code of Best Practice issued by the Committee on the Financial Aspects of Corporate Governance (the Cadbury Code).

In addition to their audit of the accounts, our external auditors have reviewed the directors' statement above concerning Vita's compliance with the Cadbury Code and their report is reproduced on page 47.

Re-appointment of directors

The Articles of Association require one-third of all directors to retire by rotation at each Annual General Meeting. Mr R. T. Scholes, Mr M. A. Jones and Mr L. D. Lawton are the three directors due to retire at this year's meeting. Mr Lawton is not seeking re-election and resolutions 3 and 4 will be proposed at the forthcoming Annual General Meeting for the re-election of Mr Scholes and Mr Jones.

Full details of the cost of the contracts, remuneration and incentive packages provided for the directors are given in the separate Remuneration Committee Report on page 20 and in Note 9 to the accounts.

Share capital

Continued enthusiasm for the Savings Related and Executive Share Option Schemes for UK and international employees resulted in 655,168 Ordinary shares being issued and allotted, fully paid, during the year. A further 91,366 shares were issued and allotted, fully paid, in response to applications in accordance with the rules of the Vita PEPs. The annual costs of administering the PEPs are met by the Company and 371 (469) individual PEP accounts were open at the end of December 1997, controlling 1,146,387 (1,271,987) Ordinary shares in the Company.

At the end of the year 221,664,926 Ordinary shares were in issue and by 9 March 1998 the number had increased to 221,693,950 through the issue of 29,024 shares in accordance with the rules of the share option schemes.

Allotment authority

The directors maintain a margin of authorised but unissued share capital, which the directors may allot pursuant to an authority granted by shareholders. Whilst there is no current intention to make any such allotment, the directors believe that it is in the best interests of the Company to renew this authority. Accordingly, Resolution 7 will be proposed at the forthcoming Annual General Meeting to renew the authority until the conclusion of the next Annual General Meeting or, if earlier, 15 July 1999, with the intention

DIRECTORS' REPORT (continued)

thereafter of renewing it at future Annual General Meetings. After taking account of the shares reserved to satisfy outstanding share options, this authority would permit the directors to allot shares up to an aggregate nominal value of £17.2m which represents 31% of the issued Ordinary share capital of the Company at 9 March 1998.

Disapplication of pre-emption rights

The Companies Act 1985 requires that any equity securities to be issued wholly for cash must first be offered to existing shareholders in proportion to their existing holdings, although this requirement may be disapplied by resolution of the shareholders. Such a disapplication is necessary so as to overcome the practical difficulties relating to fractional entitlements and the making of such offers to certain overseas shareholders that arise on a rights issue and also to permit small issues for cash otherwise than by way of rights.

Accordingly, Resolution 8 will be proposed as a special resolution at the Annual General Meeting to renew the authority of the directors to allot equity securities for cash as if the pre-emption rights provided by the Companies Act 1985 did not apply. In the case of allotments other than for rights issues, the authority is limited to the allotment of Ordinary shares with an aggregate nominal value of £2.75m representing approximately 5% of the issued Ordinary share capital of the Company at 9 March 1998.

Declarable interests

On 9 March 1998, declarable interests were held in the issued Ordinary share capital of the Company by the Norwich Union Insurance Society (6.0%), FMR Corporation/Fidelity International Limited (4.1%), the Sun Life of Canada group of companies (3.9%), the Prudential Corporation (3.3%) and the Co-operative Insurance Society Limited (3.0%). Apart from the disclosures above, the directors are not aware of any other declarable interest in excess of 3%.

The Company is not a close company within the provisions of the Income and Corporation Taxes Act 1988.

Creditors payment policy

It is the Company's policy to comply with the payment terms agreed with suppliers or, where payment terms are not specifically negotiated, to adhere to suppliers' standard terms.

At 31 December 1997, the creditors outstanding represented approximately 64 days purchases.

Personnel

The decentralised management structure creates many smaller operating units and promotes a greater sense of involvement by personnel in the success and development of 'their' business. However, to keep employees aware of wider developments within Vita, the regular company newsletter, 'Vita News', is distributed to employees on all Vita sites, with details of acquisitions, new products and a range of corporate information, together with a range of articles of a more social nature. 'Vita News' also includes extracts from the Annual Report and Accounts and the Interim Report, even though copies of both documents are also made available to all employees.

Employee involvement in the overall performance of Vita has been encouraged by promoting participation in the employee share option schemes since the first scheme was established in 1974. An approved savings related scheme has been operating, with Inland Revenue and shareholders' approval, since 1981 and a similar scheme was created in 1990 to extend the benefits to international employees. Executive share option schemes have also operated, with Inland Revenue and shareholders' approval, since 1975. The extent of employee participation in the individual schemes is detailed in note 20 to the accounts.

Vita currently has a two year service requirement for participation in the Savings Related Share Option Schemes but, in order to encourage wider participation in the Schemes, Resolution 6 will be proposed at the forthcoming Annual General Meeting to reduce the service requirement to one year.

The Vita Health & Safety and Environmental Policy and that of the appropriate individual site have been distributed to all employees, and are monitored by local and Corporate Health & Safety Committees with the objective of increasing awareness and further improving competence levels on health and safety matters.

Well-established consultative committee arrangements are actively maintained, together with collective bargaining procedures with recognised Trade Unions. Vita operates a totally non-discriminatory employment policy, part of which is the proper consideration of all applications for employment from disabled persons.

The Board is very aware of both the commercial and social importance of training its employees and utilises an increasingly wide variety of internal and external facilities to improve the effectiveness with which staff, at all levels, undertake their duties and for career development and promotion, consistent with their own abilities and the needs of their employing company.

Donations

Charitable donations made during the year amounted to £77,964, being the aggregate of a large number of normally modest donations by separate Vita companies in support of local appeals. No political donations were made during the year.

Auditors

A resolution proposing the re-appointment of Arthur Andersen as auditors of the Company will be put to the Annual General Meeting.

By order of the Board
A. R. Teague Secretary
9 March 1998

The Remuneration Committee is comprised wholly of the non-executive members of the Main Board, Messrs. Jones, Lawton, Scholes and Mr McGee as Chairman, with the Chief Executive attending, as appropriate, to give advice.

The Committee has held a number of formal, minuted, meetings during the year in accordance with well established procedures to review the remuneration package of directors and senior executives, which it believes to be in full compliance with the provisions of Section A of the best practice provisions annexed to the Stock Exchange Listing Rules. In addition, full consideration has been given to recommendations of Section B of the same best practice provisions in the formulation of current policy.

Executive directors and Management Board members for whom this Committee is responsible receive a basic salary, a performance related annual incentive, executive share options and normal employment benefits including corporate contributions toward a pension entitlement. It is intended that the total remuneration package should be sufficient to attract, retain and motivate personnel of a high calibre to optimise the continued growth of the organisation, for the benefit of all stakeholders. External comparisons are obtained from a number of sources, including independent consultants' reports and surveys.

Executive directors without a specific portfolio responsibility each receive an annual cash incentive of up to 0.15% of Vita's pre-tax profits for full attainment of specific and testing profit targets for the year, set in advance by the Committee. No incentive is payable for achievement of less than 85% of the target and potential benefits from exceeding the target are capped. Executive directors with a specific portfolio responsibility have half of their incentive based on the above method and half on the business specific basis applied to Management Board members. Typically, Management Board members are targeted to receive up to 40% of basic salary for achievement of similarly testing profit targets,

with a minimum two-thirds performance threshold and maximum cost safeguards.

Grants of share options to executive directors are at the discretion of the Committee and those to senior executives are on the recommendation of the Chief Executive. All grants are intended to promote a longer term involvement in the well-being of the Company and capital growth benefits for option holders. Options are not routinely granted on an annual basis but made on an individual basis to reflect performance, increased responsibilities and promotions.

The Board supports the institutional shareholders' requirement that the exercise of options under the new scheme should be dependent on the achievement of performance criteria pre-determined by this Committee. It is proposed that any options granted under the scheme in 1998 may not be exercised until a period of three consecutive years has elapsed during which the cumulative growth in normalised earnings per share, as published in the annual or interim results of the Company, exceeds by at least 6% the growth in the Retail Prices Index over the same period and the actual normalised earnings per share in the third year of the period is no less than that in the preceding year. The Remuneration Committee is satisfied that this is currently an appropriate measure of performance for executives of the Company.

The details of the corporate pension arrangements are explained in Note 10 to the accounts and the executives for whom the Committee is responsible participate in the main 'SE & D' scheme, with an element of increased funding to allow for enhanced early retirement options for Main and Management Board members. Additional contributions are also made to money-purchase arrangements on behalf of certain individuals.

The Committee has agreed that, whenever possible, contracts for new Board executive appointments will be on the basis of one year notice, though any internal appointments will take existing contract terms into consideration.

Mr Mercer has a two year notice entitlement and the contract for Mr O'Connor provides for one year notice, increased to two years in the event of change of control. Mr Bhatt and Mr Eaton now have fixed term contracts which, unless extended, will expire on their sixtieth birthdays in March and July 1999 respectively.

The non-executive directors all have letters of appointment for terms of office as follows:
Mr R. McGee – One year to end of June 1998, terminable by either party on 6 months notice.
Mr L. D. Lawton – One year to April 1998, expiring at the close of the forthcoming Annual General Meeting.
Mr M. A. Jones – Two years to April 1999, terminable by either party on 3 months notice.
Mr R. T. Scholes – $2^1/_2$ years to April 1998, terminable by either party on 3 months notice. It is proposed that subject to his re-election by shareholders, Mr Scholes be offered an additional term of two years.

The detailed breakdown, by element and director, of their remuneration package is given in Note 9 to the accounts.

Directors' interests

The interests of the directors in the Ordinary share capital of the Company and details of their interests in share options as at 31 December 1997 are given in Note 20 to the accounts.

Throughout the year no director had any significant interest in any contract or arrangement entered into by the Company or its subsidiary or associated undertakings.

R. McGee CBE Chairman –
Remuneration Committee
9 March 1998

ACCOUNTING POLICIES

There have been no changes to the Group's accounting policies during the year.

1. Basis of accounts The accounts are prepared under the historical cost convention modified to include the revaluation of certain fixed assets and have been prepared in accordance with applicable accounting standards.

2. Basis of consolidation The consolidated accounts include the accounts of the Company and its subsidiary undertakings and the Group's share of the results and post-acquisition reserves of associated undertakings. The results of the associated undertakings, adjusted as appropriate to accord with Group accounting policies, are included on the basis of audited accounts for a period ending not more than three months before 31 December. The net assets of subsidiary undertakings acquired during the year are incorporated at their fair value at the date of acquisition. Investments in associated undertakings acquired during the year are incorporated at the Group's share of fair value of underlying net assets at the date of acquisition. Any goodwill arising on acquisition is dealt with through distributable reserves.

Unless otherwise stated, the acquisition method of accounting has been adopted. Under this method, the results of subsidiary and associated undertakings acquired or disposed of in the year, including businesses acquired as major asset purchases, are included in the consolidated profit and loss account from the date of acquisition or up to the date of disposal.

In the Company's accounts, investments in subsidiary undertakings are stated at cost less amounts written off. Only dividends received and receivable are credited to the Company's profit and loss account.

No profit and loss account is presented for the Company as provided by section 230 of the Companies Act 1985.

3. Foreign currency The results of overseas subsidiary and associated undertakings are translated into sterling using the average rates of exchange during the year. Foreign currency assets and liabilities are translated at year end closing exchange rates. Differences arising on translation of the opening balance sheets of subsidiary and associated undertakings and retained profit for the year at the closing rate of exchange are dealt with through reserves, including differences on related foreign currency borrowings to finance the overseas investments. All other exchange differences are included in the profit and loss account.

4. Stocks are valued at the lower of first-in, first-out cost and net realisable value; cost includes appropriate production overhead expenses.

5. Turnover represents the net amounts invoiced to external customers but excludes value added and sales taxes and any part of the sales of associated undertakings.

6. Leases Assets held under finance leases are capitalised as tangible fixed assets at fair value and the corresponding rentals liability is shown net of interest under finance leases within creditors. The capitalised values are written off over the shorter of the period of the lease and the useful life of the asset concerned and finance charges are written off over the period of the lease. Rental costs under operating leases are charged to the profit and loss account over the period of the lease.

7. Depreciation of tangible fixed assets is provided at rates estimated to write off the cost or valuation of assets over their useful lives, the principal rates of annual straight line depreciation being:

a) Freehold buildings 2.5%. Freehold land is not depreciated.

b) Leasehold land and buildings 2.5% or over the period of the lease if less than forty years.

c) Plant between 10% and 33.33%.

d) Vehicles between 16% and 25%.

8. Grants on assets are credited to the profit and loss account over the lives of the relevant assets. Other grants are credited to revenue in the year in which the expenditure to which they relate is charged.

9. Research and development, patents and trade marks expenditure is charged against profit of the year in which it is incurred.

10. Pension costs in the year represent

contributions payable under money purchase schemes and, in the case of final salary related schemes, the estimated regular cost of the benefits accruing during the year, adjusted to spread any variations from regular cost over the expected remaining working lives of employees on a straight line basis. Differences between pension costs and contributions paid are recorded as assets or liabilities in the balance sheet.

11. Deferred taxation is provided using the liability method in respect of timing differences except where the liability is not expected to arise in the foreseeable future. Advance corporation tax which is available to reduce the corporation tax payable on future profits is carried forward where recovery is reasonably assured and, to the extent appropriate, is deducted from the provision for deferred taxation.

CONSOLIDATED PROFIT AND LOSS ACCOUNT
for the year ended 31 December 1997

	Notes	1997 Continuing operations	Acquisitions	Total	£m 1996
					Total
Turnover	1	800.4	8.0	808.4	895.8
Cost of sales		(605.6)	(6.5)	(612.1)	(697.1)
Gross profit		194.8	1.5	196.3	198.7
Distribution costs		(51.9)	(0.2)	(52.1)	(55.6)
Administrative expenses		(88.1)	(0.6)	(88.7)	(94.1)
Operating profit	3	54.8	0.7	55.5	49.0
Share of profits of associated undertakings	4	9.6	–	9.6	8.3
Net operating income		64.4	0.7	65.1	57.3
Closure, restructuring and disposal costs		–	–	–	(7.6)
Less 1995 provision		–	–	–	7.5
Profit on ordinary activities before interest		64.4	0.7	65.1	57.2
Net interest receivable	5	1.2	(0.1)	1.1	–
Profit on ordinary activities before taxation		65.6	0.6	66.2	57.2
Tax on profit on ordinary activities	6	(22.0)	(0.2)	(22.2)	(20.0)
Profit on ordinary activities after taxation		43.6	0.4	44.0	37.2
Minority interests	22	(0.2)	–	(0.2)	(0.3)
Profit for the financial year		43.4	0.4	43.8	36.9
Dividends	7			(19.4)	(18.2)
Retained profit for the year	21			24.4	18.7
Earnings per Ordinary share	8	19.6p	0.2p	19.8p	16.8p
Earnings per Ordinary share on continuing operations	8			19.8p	17.2p

The statement of movement in reserves is given in note 21.

Notes on pages 22, 23 and 28 to 44 form part of these accounts.

STATEMENT OF TOTAL RECOGNISED GAINS AND LOSSES
for the year ended 31 December 1997

	Notes	1997	£m 1996
Profit for the financial year		43.8	36.9
Unrealised surplus on revelation of properties		–	1.5
Currency translation differences on foreign currency net investments	21	(14.4)	(27.4)
Total recognised gains relating to the year		29.4	11.0
Note of historical cost profits and losses			
for the year ended 31 December 1997			
Reported profit on ordinary activities before taxation		66.2	57.2
Realised property revaluation gains of previous years		0.7	–
Actual depreciation charge for revalued assets		3.1	3.8
Historical cost depreciation charge for revalued assets		(2.9)	(2.8)
Historical cost profit on ordinary activities before taxation		67.1	58.2
Taxation	6	(22.2)	(20.0)
Minority interests	22	(0.2)	(0.3)
Dividends	7	(19.4)	(18.2)
Historical cost profit for the financial year retained		25.3	19.7
Reconciliation of movements in shareholders' funds			
for the year ended 31 December 1997			
Profit for the financial year		43.8	36.9
Dividends	7	(19.4)	(18.2)
		24.4	18.7
Other recognised gains and losses relating to the year (net)		(14.4)	(25.9)
New share capital subscribed		1.2	2.3
Goodwill on acquisitions during the year	12	(14.8)	(5.6)
Goodwill in Spartech	12	(8.3)	(1.3)
Net decrease in shareholders' funds		(11.9)	(11.8)
Opening shareholders' funds		298.0	309.8
Closing shareholders' funds		286.1	298.0

The movement in the shareholders' funds of the Company from £179.5m to £181.6m comprises retained profit for the financial year of £0.9m and new share capital including premium subscribed of £1.2m.

Notes on pages 22, 23 and 28 to 44 form part of these accounts.

British Vita PLC   Annual Report & Accounts 1997

BALANCE SHEETS
as at 31 December 1997

£m

	Notes	Group 1997	Group 1996	Company 1997	Company 1996
Fixed assets					
Tangible assets	11	**225.8**	229.8	**0.1**	0.2
Investments	12	**18.8**	22.4	**148.8**	134.7
		244.6	252.2	**148.9**	134.9
Current assets					
Stocks	13	**75.1**	76.4	**–**	–
Debtors falling due within one year	14	**159.5**	159.7	**38.9**	38.2
Debtors falling due after more than one year	14	**2.0**	2.0	**2.5**	2.5
Cash at bank and short term investments	15	**60.0**	55.1	**46.2**	35.3
		296.6	293.2	**87.6**	76.0
Creditors: amounts falling due within one year					
Borrowings	16	**(21.9)**	(19.8)	**(16.0)**	(1.9)
Others	16	**(179.0)**	(182.7)	**(15.6)**	(14.3)
		(200.9)	(202.5)	**(31.6)**	(16.2)
Net current assets		**95.7**	90.7	**56.0**	59.8
Total assets less current liabilities		**340.3**	342.9	**204.9**	194.7
Creditors: amounts falling due after more than one year					
Borrowings	17	**(30.1)**	(19.0)	**(20.8)**	(12.6)
Others	17	**(4.3)**	(2.7)	**(2.5)**	(2.6)
		(34.4)	(21.7)	**(23.3)**	(15.2)
Provisions for liabilities and charges	19	**(18.7)**	(22.2)	**–**	–
Net assets		**287.2**	299.0	**181.6**	179.5
Capital and reserves					
Called up share capital	20	**55.4**	55.3	**55.4**	55.3
Share premium account	21	**92.0**	90.9	**92.0**	90.9
Revaluation reserve	21	**15.6**	17.3	**–**	–
Other reserves	21	**3.2**	3.4	**9.4**	9.4
Profit and loss account	21	**119.9**	131.1	**24.8**	23.9
Shareholders' funds (including non-equity interests)		**286.1**	298.0	**181.6**	179.5
Minority interests	22	**1.1**	1.0	**–**	–
Total capital employed		**287.2**	299.0	**181.6**	179.5

The accounts on pages 22 to 44 were approved by the Board on 9 March 1998 and were signed on its behalf by:

R. McGee CBE
J. Mercer
C. J. O'Connor   Directors

Notes on pages 22, 23 and 28 to 44 form part of these accounts.

British Vita PLC   Annual Report & Accounts 1997

CASH FLOW STATEMENT
for the year ended 31 December 1997

	Notes	1997	£m 1996
Net cash inflow from operating activities	24	**74.0**	88.7
Returns on investments and servicing of finance			
Interest received		**3.4**	2.5
Interest paid		**(1.7)**	(2.7)
Interest element of finance lease rentals		**(0.2)**	(0.3)
Dividends received from associated undertakings		**1.5**	1.2
Minority interests		**(0.1)**	(0.1)
Net cash inflow from returns on investments and servicing of finance		**2.9**	0.6
Taxation paid		**(15.6)**	(14.1)
Capital expenditure			
Purchase of tangible fixed assets		**(38.6)**	(38.0)
Sale of tangible fixed assets		**5.6**	4.3
Investment grants received		**0.1**	0.1
Net cash outflow from capital expenditure		**(32.9)**	(33.6)
Acquisitions and disposals			
Purchase of subsidiary undertakings	12	**(19.4)**	(34.9)
Purchase of associated undertakings	12	**(0.5)**	–
Sale of subsidiary undertakings		**–**	7.2
Sale of associated undertakings		**–**	12.4
Other investments		**–**	(1.9)
Net cash outflow from acquisitions		**(19.9)**	(17.2)
Equity dividends paid		**(18.8)**	(17.6)
Cash (outflow) inflow before use of liquid resources and financing		**(10.3)**	6.8
Management of liquid resources			
Increase in non-cash equivalent deposits and short-term investments	26	**(9.8)**	(4.4)
Net cash outflow from management of liquid resources		**(9.8)**	(4.4)
Financing			
Issue of Ordinary share capital		**1.2**	2.3
Net increase in loans		**16.3**	0.3
Capital element of finance lease rentals		**(0.2)**	(0.3)
Net cash inflow from financing		**17.3**	2.3
(Decrease) increase in cash in the year	26	**(2.8)**	4.7

Notes on pages 22, 23 and 28 to 44 form part of these accounts.

British Vita PLC   Annual Report & Accounts 1997

NOTES TO THE ACCOUNTS

£m

1 Segmental analysis		Turnover		Operating profit		Net assets
	1997	1996	1997	1996	1997	1996
Class of business		Restated		Restated		Restated
Cellular polymers	459.7	505.1	32.1	27.2	143.4	143.5
Industrial polymers	200.3	207.4	15.7	15.6	70.0	65.0
Fibres and fabrics	148.4	161.0	7.7	7.1	45.8	50.1
	808.4	873.5	55.5	49.9	259.2	258.6
Discontinued activities	–	22.3	–	(0.9)	–	0.7
	808.4	895.8	55.5	49.0	259.2	259.3
Geographical origin						
United Kingdom	351.9	349.4	30.0	24.1	96.5	91.9
Continental Europe	362.0	438.6	20.8	22.0	119.3	133.2
International	94.5	85.5	4.7	3.8	43.4	33.5
	808.4	873.5	55.5	49.9	259.2	258.6
Discontinued activities	–	22.3	–	(0.9)	–	0.7
	808.4	895.8	55.5	49.0	259.2	259.3
Geographical destination						
United Kingdom	303.3	304.4				
Benelux	48.3	60.0				
France	122.0	142.5				
Germany	124.3	162.8				
Other	101.8	103.9				
Continental Europe	396.4	469.2				
International	108.7	99.9				
	808.4	873.5				
Discontinued activities	–	22.3				
	808.4	895.8				

Discontinued activities in 1996 incurred £20.2m for cost of sales, £1.4m for distribution costs and £1.6m for administrative expenses.

Net assets comprise shareholders' funds, excluding investments, cash and borrowings.

2 Exchange rates
The principal exchange rates used in the preparation of the accounts are:

	Average			Year end		
	1997	1996	% Change	1997	1996	% Change
Belgium	58.53	48.39	21.0%	60.96	54.35	12.2%
France	9.55	7.99	19.5%	9.90	8.90	11.2%
Germany	2.84	2.35	20.9%	2.96	2.64	12.1%
The Netherlands	3.19	2.63	21.3%	3.34	2.96	12.8%
United States	1.64	1.56	5.1%	1.65	1.71	(3.5%)

British Vita PLC　　Annual Report & Accounts 1997

(172)

		£m
3 Operating profit	**1997**	1996
is stated after charging (crediting):		
Depreciation of tangible fixed assets		
– owned	**27.1**	30.9
– held under finance leases	**0.2**	0.2
Operating leases	**3.1**	3.3
Auditors' remuneration	**0.7**	0.8
Research and development	**2.4**	2.4
Government grants	**(0.2)**	(0.3)
Employment costs	**181.1**	201.8

The Group auditors also received £0.2m (£0.2m) in respect of non-audit services.

4 Share of associated undertakings		
Share of turnover	**122.9**	121.1
Share of profits	**9.6**	8.3
Taxation (note 6)	**(3.4)**	(3.0)
	6.2	5.3
Less receivable as dividends	**(1.6)**	(1.0)
Retained by associated undertakings (note 12)	**4.6**	4.3
5 Net interest receivable		
Bank overdrafts, acceptance credits and bank loans	**(2.0)**	(2.2)
Finance leases	**(0.2)**	(0.3)
Other loans	**(0.1)**	(0.1)
	(2.3)	(2.6)
Less interest receivable	**3.4**	2.6
	1.1	–

Included in the above is interest paid by discontinued activities of £Nil (£0.2m) relating to bank overdrafts.

6 Tax on profit on ordinary activities		
UK Corporation tax at 31.5% (33%)		
– continuing activities	**10.0**	9.3
– acquisitions	**0.1**	–
Overseas tax		
– continuing activities before exceptional items	**9.0**	7.8
– acquisitions	**0.1**	1.1
– discontinued activities	**–**	(0.3)
Associated undertakings (note 4)	**3.4**	3.0
Deferred taxation (note 19)	**(0.4)**	(0.9)
	22.2	20.0

		£m
7 Dividends	**1997**	1996
Ordinary shares:		
Interim paid at 4.25p (4.0p) per share	**9.4**	8.8
Final proposed at 4.5p (4.25p) per share	**10.0**	9.4
	19.4	18.2
8 Earnings per Ordinary share		
Profit for the financial year on continuing operations before		
exceptional items and after preference dividend	**43.4**	36.0
Acquisitions	**0.4**	1.8
	43.8	37.8
Net loss on discontinued operations	**–**	(0.9)
Net profit for the financial year	**43.8**	36.9
Weighted average number of Ordinary shares in issue (millions)	**221.2**	220.2
Earnings per Ordinary share	**19.8p**	16.8p
Earnings per Ordinary share on continuing operations before exceptional items	**19.8p**	17.2p

The directors consider that the earnings per share calculated on the basis of continuing activities before exceptional items and discontinued operations gives a better understanding of the Group's earnings.

9 Employment costs		
Employees and directors:		
Wages and salaries	**150.5**	166.0
Social security costs	**23.7**	28.8
Other pension costs	**6.9**	7.0
	181.1	201.8

	1997	1996
Average numbers employed:		
UK	**4,282**	4,273
Continental Europe	**3,621**	4,073
International	**1,606**	1,564
Company and subsidiary undertakings	**9,509**	9,910
Associated undertakings	**4,089**	3,305
	13,598	13,215

9 Employment costs (continued)

Directors' remuneration

	Executive salary/fees	Performance incentive	Benefits	Money purchase contributions	Share option gains	1997 Total £	1996 Total (restated) £
Mr R. McGee	60,000	–	976	–	681	61,657	61,737
Mr J. Mercer	184,055	109,900	14,827	6,535	–	315,317	250,805
Mr F. J. Eaton	176,730	91,650	12,823	–	144	281,347	252,689
Mr K. R. Bhatt	131,555	73,400	9,734	–	144	214,833	192,607
Mr M. A. Jones	23,950	–	–	–	–	23,950	23,250
Mr L. D. Lawton	30,000	–	1,959	–	–	31,959	34,278
Mr F. J. Libeert	153,546	41,230	10,035	–	–	204,811	257,835
Mr C. J. O'Connor	124,426	73,400	7,747	10,935	–	216,508	98,244
Mr R. T. Scholes*	23,950	–	–	–	–	23,950	23,250
Mr R. H. Sellers	102,527	–	32,477	656	21,833	157,493	301,696
Total	1,010,739	389,580	90,578	18,126	22,802	1,531,825	–
Prior year total	1,020,629	399,627	62,412	10,536	3,187	–	1,496,391

Prior year figures are restated to eliminate final salary pension costs, now covered by separate disclosure, and to include share option gains.

Mr Libeert's costs include conversion of the foreign currency payments at the average exchange rate during the month in which they were paid.

In addition to his emoluments shown above, Mr Sellers was paid £260,000 by the Company as compensation for loss of office as a director following his resignation from the Board on 30 June 1997.

* Payment in respect of Mr Scholes' service was made to Kleinwort Benson Securities Limited.

In addition to the above payments, pensions payable to former directors or their dependants were £16,417 (£15,932).

Directors' pension entitlements

	Increase in accrued pension excluding inflation £	Net transfer value of increase £	Accrued pension 31 December 1997 (or earlier termination) £	Accrued pension 31 December 1997 £
Mr J. Mercer	14,259	177,454	82,615	66,950
Mr F. J. Eaton	3,814	47,720	114,067	107,985
Mr K. R. Bhatt	5,749	83,048	84,927	77,549
Mr C. J. O'Connor	1,725	10,813	2,586	843
Mr R. H. Sellers	8,294	143,261	102,674	94,380

The pension entitlement shown is that which would be paid annually on retirement based on service to the end of the year or for Mr Sellers the date of leaving. The increase in accrued pension during the year excludes any increase for inflation.

The transfer value has been calculated on the basis of actuarial advice in accordance with Actuarial Guidance Note GN11 less directors' contributions.

Members of the scheme have the option to pay Additional Voluntary Contributions; neither the contributions nor the resulting benefits are included in the above table.

Three directors are also members of money purchase arrangements. For Mr O'Connor this relates to the element of salary over the Earnings Cap and, for Mr Mercer and Mr Sellers, to a proportion of their salary, deemed by the Remuneration Committee to be eligible for money purchase benefits only. Contributions paid by the Company in respect of such directors are shown in the remuneration analysis above.

Life assurance is also provided for all executive directors at four times annual basic salary.

NOTES TO THE ACCOUNTS (continued)

9 Employment costs (continued)

The pension entitlement for Mr Libeert is arranged in Belgium through an insurer on a final salary/ money purchase hybrid basis to provide a cash sum on retirement using a formula based on service and salary at retirement. At 31 December 1997, the accrued cash sum benefit was Bfr12m compared to the prior year benefit of Bfr10m, being an increase in the cash sum accrued of Bfr1.3m after excluding increase for inflation.

10 Pension arrangements

Vita companies continue to provide pension benefits for many employees by contributing to a variety of pension arrangements in addition to those provided by the State. In compliance with the Statement of Standard Accounting Practice No.24 (SSAP 24) 'Accounting for Pension Costs', the cost of these additional benefits is charged to the profit and loss account in the year in which it is incurred. Any difference between this charge and the actual contributions payable to external funds is shown on the balance sheet as an asset or liability.

Within the UK, the majority of employees are eligible to join one of two schemes administered by British Vita Pension Fund Trustees Limited and British Vita 'SE & D' Pension Fund Trustees Limited, which provide final salary related benefits from separately invested assets. The schemes are funded in accordance with the recommendations of the consultant actuaries, William M. Mercer Limited. The members of the schemes are contracted-in to the State Earnings Related Pension Scheme but members have the option of contracting-out via a Rebate Only Personal Pension Scheme. All members receive an annual benefits statement, together with a copy of an annual report on the status of the appropriate scheme.

An actuarial valuation is undertaken every two years and the last valuation was performed at 31 March 1996 using the projected unit method to be consistent with the method used for the SSAP 24 valuation. The schemes were funded to a level between 116% and 124% of the accrued liabilities at the date of the valuation, after allowing for anticipated increases in remuneration levels. The major assumptions were dividend growth of 4.5%, an interest rate of 9% and an allowance for general earnings inflation of 7% per annum. The two schemes held investments with a market value of £158m at 31 March 1997, including 1,960,692 Ordinary shares of British Vita PLC which then represented approximately 2.6% of the schemes' assets. The level of 'self-investment' was reduced in October 1997 by the sale of 650,000 shares. The main Vita schemes provide between 3% and 5% guaranteed indexation of current pensions, indexation in line with retail price index to a maximum of 5% of deferred pensions and apply equalised provisions for men and women.

Money-purchase schemes are operated in France, Belgium and Australia and employer contributions to these schemes are charged to the profit and loss account in the year in which they are payable. Companies in the Netherlands operate final salary schemes, the liabilities of which are substantially insured.

A number of unfunded schemes are operated in Germany providing fixed amounts or final salary related benefits, for which reserves are created in accordance with the recommendations of the consultant actuary, International Pension Consultants GmbH. Actuarial valuations are normally undertaken annually on the projected unit method based on the major assumption of a 6.0% per annum interest rate. Full provision has been made for the results of the last valuation, undertaken as of 31 December 1997.

Calculations have been performed for all final salary related schemes to comply with SSAP 24 using the projected unit method with similar assumptions to the main biennial valuations. It is the objective to fund pension arrangements by a substantially level contribution rate. The total pension charge for the year was £6.9m (£7.0m) after deducting £0.3m (£0.1m) in respect of the amortisation of surpluses arising over the average remaining service lives of employees in the various schemes.

11 Tangible fixed assets

	Land & buildings	Group Plant & vehicles	Total	£m Company Plant & vehicles
Cost or valuation				
Balance 31 December 1996	117.6	316.0	433.6	0.3
Exchange rate adjustments	(7.5)	(20.1)	(27.6)	–
Additions	10.3	27.0	37.3	–
New subsidiary undertakings	1.9	4.3	6.2	–
Disposals	(3.8)	(16.0)	(19.8)	–
Balance 31 December 1997*	**118.5**	**311.2**	**429.7**	**0.3**
Accumulated depreciation				
Balance 31 December 1996	–	203.8	203.8	0.1
Exchange rate adjustments	(0.1)	(14.3)	(14.4)	–
New subsidiary undertakings	0.3	1.6	1.9	–
Disposals	(0.1)	(14.6)	(14.7)	–
Charge for year	3.1	24.2	27.3	0.1
Balance 31 December 1997	**3.2**	**200.7**	**203.9**	**0.2**
Net book value				
31 December 1997	**115.3**	**110.5**	**225.8**	**0.1**
31 December 1996	117.6	112.2	229.8	0.2
*Cost and valuation analysis:				
Valuation 1996	106.3	–	106.3	–
Cost	12.2	311.2	323.4	0.3
	118.5	311.2	429.7	0.3
Land and buildings comprise:				
Freehold	112.9			
Long leasehold buildings	2.2			
Buildings subject to finance leases	3.4			
	118.5			

If land and buildings had not been revalued they would have been included at cost of £124.3m (£123.3m) less accumulated depreciation of £23.6m (£22.8m). Land at cost and valuation of £22.5m (£23.6m) is not depreciated.

£m

12 Investments	Group				Company		
	Associated undertakings		Other invest-		Subsidiary under-	Associated under-	
	Listed	Unlisted	ments	Total	takings	takings	Total
Shares at cost less amounts written off							
Balance 31 December 1996	**10.5**	**0.4**	**1.9**	**12.8**	**114.7**	**0.2**	**114.9**
Exchange rate adjustments	**0.4**	**(0.1)**	**(0.2)**	**0.1**	**-**	**-**	**-**
Additions	**0.5**	**-**	**-**	**0.5**	**5.4**	**-**	**5.4**
Balance 31 December 1997	**11.4**	**0.3**	**1.7**	**13.4**	**120.1**	**0.2**	**120.3**
Share of post acquisition reserves							
Balance 31 December 1996	**2.5**	**7.0**	**-**	**9.5**	**-**	**-**	**-**
Exchange rate adjustments	**(0.4)**	**(0.1)**	**-**	**(0.5)**	**-**	**-**	**-**
Goodwill adjustment Spartech*	**(8.3)**	**-**	**-**	**(8.3)**	**-**	**-**	**-**
Share of retained profits for the year	**4.4**	**0.2**	**-**	**4.6**	**-**	**-**	**-**
Balance 31 December 1997	**(1.8)**	**7.1**	**-**	**5.3**	**-**	**-**	**-**
Loans							
Balance 31 December 1996	**-**	**0.1**	**-**	**0.1**	**19.7**	**0.1**	**19.8**
Exchange rate adjustments	**-**	**-**	**-**	**-**	**(1.7)**	**-**	**(1.7)**
Advances	**-**	**-**	**-**	**-**	**11.3**	**-**	**11.3**
Repayments	**-**	**-**	**-**	**-**	**(0.9)**	**-**	**(0.9)**
Balance 31 December 1997	**-**	**0.1**	**-**	**0.1**	**28.4**	**0.1**	**28.5**
Net book value							
31 December 1997	**9.6**	**7.5**	**1.7**	**18.8**	**148.5**	**0.3**	**148.8**
31 December 1996	13.0	7.5	1.9	22.4	134.4	0.3	134.7

* The Common Stock holding in Spartech Corporation was 33.2% (33.1%).
In accordance with Group accounting policy, goodwill of £8.3m arising on the acquisition of Preferred
Plastic Sheet Division has been dealt with through reserves.

The market value of shares listed overseas and directors' valuation of unlisted shares in associated
undertakings is:

31 December 1997	**81.8**	**8.8**	**1.7**	**92.3**	**-**	**-**	**-**
31 December 1996	57.6	8.8	1.9	68.3	-	0.8	0.8

	£m
12 Investments (continued)	Business and subsidiary undertakings
Details of acquisitions during the year are as follows:	Acquired
	Fair values
Tangible fixed assets and investments	**4.3**
Current assets:	
Stocks	**1.9**
Debtors	**4.7**
Cash at bank and in hand	**4.5**
Creditors due within one year:	
Bank overdrafts	**(0.1)**
Trade creditors	**(2.1)**
Other creditors and accruals	**(3.3)**
Minority interest acquired	**(0.9)**
Net assets acquired	**9.0**
Consideration paid:	
Cash	**23.0**
Costs of acquisitions	**0.2**
Deferred consideration	**0.6**
Total	**23.8**
Goodwill on acquisitions (note 21)	**14.8**

Analysis of the net outflow of cash in respect of the acquisitions of subsidiary undertakings:

Cash consideration	**23.8**
Cash at bank and in hand	**(4.5)**
Bank overdrafts	**0.1**
	19.4

The only fair value adjustment recorded was to reflect the fair market value of land and buildings. This resulted in an uplift to the book value acquired of £0.2m in respect of the business.

13 Stocks	**Group**		**Company**	
	1997	1996	**1997**	1996
Raw materials and consumable stores	**42.6**	42.9	**–**	–
Work in progress and finished goods	**32.5**	33.5	**–**	–
	75.1	76.4	**–**	–

NOTES TO THE ACCOUNTS (continued)

£m

14 Debtors	Group		Company	
	1997	1996	1997	1996
Amounts falling due within one year				
Trade debtors	140.8	140.5	–	–
Amounts owed by subsidiary undertakings	–	–	35.8	34.8
Amounts owed by associated undertakings	0.8	0.8	0.1	0.1
Other debtors	9.6	9.3	–	0.2
Prepayments and accrued income	8.3	9.1	0.4	0.3
Advance corporation tax	–	–	2.6	2.8
	159.5	159.7	38.9	38.2
Amounts falling due after more than one year				
Other debtors	0.8	0.6	–	–
Recoverable taxation	1.2	1.4	2.5	2.5
	2.0	2.0	2.5	2.5
15 Cash and short term investments				
Cash at bank	17.5	22.4	10.5	12.1
Term deposits	42.5	32.7	35.7	23.2
	60.0	55.1	46.2	35.3

Term deposits represent cash on deposit with banks for periods in excess of twenty four hours.

16 Creditors: amounts falling due within one year				
Borrowings				
Current portion of secured loans	5.0	5.9	–	–
Current portion of unsecured loans	2.8	3.3	–	–
Loans falling due within one year (note 18)	7.8	9.2	–	–
Bank overdrafts and acceptance credits – unsecured	7.1	8.3	11.3	1.2
Bank overdrafts and acceptance credits – secured	1.9	1.3	–	–
Loan notes – unsecured	4.7	0.7	4.7	0.7
Finance leases	0.4	0.3	–	–
	21.9	19.8	16.0	1.9
Others				
Trade creditors	99.6	99.7	–	–
Bills payable	6.6	8.9	–	–
Amounts owed to subsidiary undertakings	–	–	0.2	–
Amounts owed to associated undertakings	0.1	0.2	–	–
Corporation tax	17.6	14.7	3.8	4.0
Other taxes and social security costs	13.2	13.8	0.1	0.1
Other creditors	6.5	6.7	0.3	0.1
Accruals and deferred income	25.4	29.3	1.2	0.7
Proposed dividend	10.0	9.4	10.0	9.4
	179.0	182.7	15.6	14.3

British Vita PLC   Annual Report & Accounts 1997

17 Creditors: amounts falling due after more than one year

	Group		Company	
	1997	1996	**1997**	1996
Borrowings				
Loans (note 18)	**28.0**	17.2	**20.8**	12.6
Finance leases	**2.1**	1.8	**–**	–
	30.1	19.0	**20.8**	12.6
Others				
Amounts owed to subsidiary undertakings	**–**	–	**2.5**	2.6
Deferred income – government grants	**0.5**	0.6	**–**	–
Other creditors	**3.8**	2.1	**–**	–
	4.3	2.7	**2.5**	2.6
Finance lease obligations payable comprise:				
between one and two years	**0.4**	0.2	**–**	–
between two and five years	**0.7**	0.6	**–**	–
beyond five years	**1.0**	1.0	**–**	–
	2.1	1.8	**–**	–

18 Loans

		Group		Company	
Long term (not wholly repayable within five years)					
Overseas					
Ffr bank loans	1997–2003	**–**	0.6	**–**	–
Sch bank loans	1997–2008	**–**	0.6	**–**	–
Medium term (repayable within five years)					
UK					
Dm bank loans	1998–2000	**12.2**	10.5	**12.2**	10.5
Ffr bank loans	1998–1999	**1.9**	2.1	**1.9**	2.1
US$ bank loans	1998–1999	**6.7**	–	**6.7**	–
Overseas					
Dm bank loans	1998–2001	**7.7**	7.5	**–**	–
Bfr bank loan	1998	**1.6**	1.7	**–**	–
DKr bank loans	1998–2001	**1.4**	2.0	**–**	–
Ffr bank loans	1998–2002	**1.0**	1.4	**–**	–
Lit bank loans	1998–1999	**3.1**	–	**–**	–
Sch bank loans	1998	**0.2**	–	**–**	–
		35.8	26.4	**20.8**	12.6
The loans are repayable as follows:					
between one and two years		**19.7**	0.9	**14.9**	–
between two and five years		**8.3**	15.8	**5.9**	12.6
beyond five years		**–**	0.5	**–**	–
Amounts falling due after more than one year (note 17)		**28.0**	17.2	**20.8**	12.6
Amounts falling due within one year (note 16)		**7.8**	9.2	**–**	–
		35.8	26.4	**20.8**	12.6

British Vita PLC   Annual Report & Accounts 1997

£m

18 Loans (continued)

Long term (not wholly repayable within five years)

Interest charges on the bank loans are linked to inter-bank rates relative to the currency borrowed.
All overseas bank loans are secured by fixed charges except for £1.3m of Dm loan, £3.1m of Lit loans,
£1.6m of the Bfr loans and £1.4m of the Dkr loans.

19 Provisions for liabilities and charges

Group	Deferred taxation	Pensions	Other	Total
Balance 31 December 1996	5.3	10.2	6.7	22.2
Exchange rate adjustments	(0.4)	(1.4)	(0.4)	(2.2)
Utilised during the year	(0.4)	0.6	(1.4)	(1.2)
Advance corporation tax	(0.1)	–	–	(0.1)
Balance 31 December 1997	**4.4**	**9.4**	**4.9**	**18.7**

'Other' relates to employment termination and business restructuring provisions.

	Group		Company	
Provision for deferred taxation	**1997**	1996	**1997**	1996
Accelerated capital allowances	6.9	7.7	–	–
Advance corporation tax recoverable	(2.5)	(2.4)	–	–
	4.4	5.3	–	–
Full potential liability for deferred taxation				
Accelerated capital allowances	8.9	10.1	–	–
Other timing differences	(0.4)	–	–	–
Advance corporation tax recoverable	(2.5)	(2.4)	–	–
	6.0	7.7	–	–

No capital gains tax provision has been made in respect of the revaluation surplus on properties which are
held for long term use.

20 Called up share capital	Authorised		£m Allotted, called up and fully paid	
	1997	1996	1997	1996
Non-equity				
4.2% Cumulative Preference shares of £1 each				
(1996 – 0.1m authorised, 0.1m allotted)	–	0.1	–	0.1
Equity				
Ordinary shares of 25p each (300.0m authorised, 221.7m allotted)	75.0	75.0	55.4	55.2
	75.0	75.1	55.4	55.3

During the year, 655,168 Ordinary shares were allotted and issued, fully paid, in accordance with the rules of the share option schemes and 91,366 Ordinary shares were allotted and issued, fully paid, to subscribers to the Vita PEPs.

In accordance with approval given by shareholders at the Annual General Meeting in 1997, the former 4.2% Cumulative Preference shares were purchased and cancelled during the year.

Employee share options

Employee participation in the Company continues to be successfully encouraged by means of share option schemes. At 31 December 1997, the British Vita Savings Related Share Option Schemes had 4,347 options outstanding over 5,349,685 shares at prices between 165.6p and 230.4p, including 1,275 options outstanding over 1,189,516 shares granted in May 1997 at 174.8p. Options under these Schemes granted prior to May 1997 are exercisable on the fifth anniversary of the grant and those since May 1997 on the third anniversary of the grant. In the ten years to December 1997, options had been exercised over 3,755,075 shares.

The Vita International Savings Related Share Option Scheme was introduced during 1990 and at 31 December 1997 there were 118 options outstanding over 203,833 shares at prices of between 165.6p and 288p, including 37 options over 33,846 shares at 174.8p and 2 options over 2,704 shares at 218.5p granted in May 1997. Options under this Scheme granted prior to May 1997 are exercisable on the fifth anniversary of the grant and those since May 1997 on the third anniversary of the grant. In the seven years to December 1997, options have been exercised over 142,654 shares.

The 1984 and 1995 British Vita Executive and International Share Option Schemes had 640 options outstanding at 31 December 1997 over 3,584,010 shares at prices between 137.902p and 294p, including 94 options over 485,000 shares granted in April 1997 at 218.5p and 24 options over 166,000 shares granted in October 1997 at 249.5p. Options under these Schemes are exercisable between the third and tenth anniversary of the grant and, in the ten years to December 1997, options had been exercised over 2,345,689 shares. Options granted in accordance with the rules of the current Scheme, approved by Shareholders at the Annual General Meeting in 1996, are also subject to the achievement of performance criteria before they can be exercised.

At 31 December 1997, a further 6,785,118 shares were available for future grants of options under all schemes.

20 Called up share capital (continued)
Directors' shareholdings

	31 December 1997			31 December 1996		
	Beneficial	Non-beneficial	Options	Beneficial	Non-beneficial	Options
R. McGee	510,123	235,025	–	580,224	85,025	4,899
J. Mercer	72,456	–	137,504	67,456	–	138,799
F. J. Eaton	415,093	98,550	17,794	468,644	48,550	18,570
K. R. Bhatt	216,503	–	42,724	202,415	–	43,759
M. A. Jones	2,000	–	–	2,000	–	–
L. D. Lawton	365,710	100,845	–	365,710	100,845	–
F. J. Libeert	151,036	–	50,000	151,036	–	50,000
C. J. O'Connor	11,000	–	25,000	2,500	–	25,000
R. T. Scholes	4,000	–	–	4,000	–	–

There has been no change in the directors' interests between 31 December 1997 and 9 March 1998.
In addition to the listed holdings, British Vita SE & D Pension Fund Trustees Limited holds 717,776
(1,042,776) Ordinary shares and British Vita Pension Fund Trustees Limited holds 592,916 (917,916)
Ordinary shares. The Boards of the Trustee companies include Mr M. A. Jones as Chairman and two other
directors of the Company.

Directors' share options outstanding

Year	Adjusted price p	R. McGee	J. Mercer	F. J. Eaton	K. R. Bhatt	F. Libeert	C. J. O'Connor	R. H. Sellers	Total
Executive scheme									
1990	179.143	–	–	–	–	–	–	31,036	31,036
1992	237.000	–	20,000	–	25,000	–	–	–	45,000
1995	149.000	–	10,000	10,000	10,000	10,000	–	10,000	50,000
1996	204.000	–	100,000	–	–	40,000	–	–	140,000
1996	219.000	–	–	–	–	–	25,000	–	25,000
Exercised		–	–	–	–	–	–	(31,036)	(31,036)
		–	130,000	10,000	35,000	50,000	25,000	10,000	260,000
Savings Related schemes									
1992	229.600	4,899	4,083	2,449	3,266	–	–	3,266	17,963
1993	177.600	–	1,359	1,554	971	–	–	621	4,505
1994	230.400	–	–	1,497	748	–	–	868	3,113
1995	204.000	–	1,691	2,029	1,691	–	–	1,691	7,102
1996	165.600	–	1,666	1,041	2,083	–	–	2,291	7,081
1997	174.800	–	2,788	1,673	2,231	–	–	–	6,692
Exercised		(4,899)	–	(2,449)	(3,266)	–	–	(468)	(11,082)
Lapsed		–	(4,083)	–	–	–	–	(8,269)	(12,352)
		–	7,504	7,794	7,724	–	–	–	23,022
Total at 31 Dec. 1997		–	137,504	17,794	42,724	50,000	25,000	10,000	283,022

Mr Sellers exercised part of his 1993 savings related options on 1 July 1997 at 210p and his executive
option on 9 September 1997 at a middle-market price of 247p, Mr Bhatt on 14 November 1997 at 234p, Mr
Eaton on 19 November 1997 at 235.5p and Mr McGee on 25 November at 243.5p.

21 Reserves

	Share premium	Revaluation reserve	Other reserves	Profit and loss	£m Total
Group					
Balance 31 December 1996	**90.9**	**17.3**	**3.4**	**131.1**	**242.7**
Exchange rate adjustments	–	**(1.0)**	**(0.6)**	**(12.8)**	**(14.4)**
Premium on issues of shares	**1.1**	–	–	–	**1.1**
Goodwill on acquisitions	–	–	–	**(14.8)**	**(14.8)**
Goodwill in Spartech	–	–	–	**(8.3)**	**(8.3)**
Realised revaluation gains	–	**(0.7)**	–	**0.7**	–
Retained profit for the year	–	–	–	**24.4**	**24.4**
Other movements	–	–	**0.4**	**(0.4)**	–
Balance 31 December 1997	**92.0**	**15.6**	**3.2**	**119.9**	**230.7**

Included in the above is the share of reserves of associated undertakings

1997	–	0.1	1.3	3.9	5.3
1996	–	0.2	1.3	8.0	9.5
Company					
Balance 31 December 1996	90.9	–	9.4	23.9	124.2
Premium on issues of shares	1.1	–	–	–	1.1
Retained profit for the year	–	–	–	0.9	0.9
Balance 31 December 1997	**92.0**	**–**	**9.4**	**24.8**	**126.2**

The cumulative amount of goodwill resulting from acquisitions in the current and earlier financial years which has been written off is £68.1m (£45.0m).

Of the total reserves shown in the balance sheets, only the profit and loss account reserves are regarded as distributable.

22 Minority interest

	1997	1996
Equity interest at beginning of the year	1.0	1.1
Exchange rate adjustment	(0.2)	(0.2)
Acquired during the year	0.9	(0.1)
Goodwill acquired	(0.7)	–
Share of retained profit after taxation	0.2	0.3
Dividends paid	(0.1)	(0.1)
Equity interest at end of the year	1.1	1.0

23 Capital and leasing commitments

Commitments for capital expenditure at 31 December 1997 contracted but not provided for in the accounts amounted to £11.7m (£6.3m) for the Group and £Nil (£Nil) for the Company.

The Group has annual commitments in respect of operating leases expiring:

	Land and buildings	Plant and vehicles
Within one year	0.5	0.7
Between one and five years	1.6	2.2
Beyond five years	0.7	0.1
	2.8	3.0

During the year the Group entered into finance lease arrangements in respect of assets with a total capital value at the inception of the leases of £0.2m (£Nil).

		£m
24 Net cash inflow from operating activities	**1997**	1996
Operating profit	**55.5**	49.0
Depreciation charges	**27.3**	31.1
Government grants	**(0.2)**	(0.3)
Profit on sale of tangible fixed assets	**(0.5)**	(1.0)
Decrease in provisions	**(0.7)**	(8.4)
(Increase) decrease in stocks	**(1.6)**	13.0
Increase in debtors	**(4.4)**	(0.1)
(Decrease) increase in creditors	**(1.4)**	5.4
Net cash inflow from operating activities	**74.0**	88.7

The acquisitions made during the year contributed £0.3m (£3.8m) to the Group's net operating cash flows, paid £0.1m (£0.1m) in respect of net returns on investment and servicing of finance, paid £0.1m (£Nil) in respect of taxation and utilised £0.2m (£0.1m) for capital expenditure.

25 Reconciliation of net cash flow to movement in net funds

(Decrease) increase in cash in the year (note 26)	**(2.8)**	4.7
Cash outflow from decrease in debt and lease financing	**(16.1)**	–
Cash outflow from increase in liquid resources	**9.8**	4.4
Change in net debt resulting from cash flows	**(9.1)**	9.1
Loans and finance leases acquired with subsidiary	**(0.8)**	(1.3)
Translation difference	**1.6**	3.9
Movement in net funds in the year	**(8.3)**	11.7
Net funds at 1 January	**16.3**	4.6
Net funds at 31 December	**8.0**	16.3

26 Analysis of net funds

	At 1 Jan 1997	Cash flow	Acquisitions	Exchange movements	At 31 Dec 1997
Cash at bank and in hand	22.4	(1.9)	–	(3.0)	17.5
Overdrafts	(9.6)	(0.9)	–	1.5	(9.0)
		(2.8)			
Loans	(27.1)	(16.3)	–	2.9	(40.5)
Finance leases	(2.1)	0.2	(0.8)	0.2	(2.5)
		(16.1)			
Term deposits	32.7	9.8	–	–	42.5
	16.3	(9.1)	(0.8)	1.6	8.0

27 Contingencies

The Company has guaranteed certain of the overdrafts and third party liabilities of certain subsidiary undertakings, amounting to £24.5m (£22.9m).

In addition to pension liabilities referred to in note 10, there were contingent liabilities in respect of discounted bills of exchange totalling £1.7m (£1.8m) for the Group.

PRINCIPAL SUBSIDIARY AND ASSOCIATED UNDERTAKINGS

Subsidiary undertakings	Country of incorporation and principal operation	Product or activities
United Kingdom		
Ball & Young Limited	England	Cellular polymer products
British Vita Investments Limited	England	Property Management
Caligen Foam Limited	England	Cellular polymer products
Jackdaw Polymers Limited	England	Polymeric compounds
Kay-Metzeler Limited	England	Cellular polymer products
H. E. Mowbray & Company Limited	England	Fibre processing
Royalite Plastics Limited	Scotland	Polymeric products
Silvergate Plastics Limited	England	Polymeric products
The Rossendale Combining Company Limited	England	Specialised textiles
Vitacom Limited	England	Polymeric compounds
Vitafoam Limited	England	Cellular polymer products
Vitafibres Limited	England	Fibre processing
Vitamol Limited	England	Polymeric products
Vita Industrial Polymers Limited	England	Polymeric products
Vita Liquid Polymers Limited	England	Polymeric compounds
Vita International Limited	England	Parent company
Vita International Investments Limited	England	Parent company
Vita Services Limited	England	Administrative services
Vita Thermoplastic Compounds Limited	England	Polymeric compounds
Vita-tex Limited	England	Specialised textiles
Continental Europe		
Caligen Europe BV	Netherlands	Cellular polymer products
Deutsche Vita Polymere GmbH	Germany	Parent company
Draka Interfoam BV	Netherlands	Cellular polymer products
Gaillon SA	France	Polymeric products
ICOA France SA	France	Cellular polymer products
SA Isofel (78.4%)	Spain	Cellular polymer products
Jackdaw Polymeres SA	France	Polymeric compounds
Koepp AG (94.25%)	Germany	Cellular polymer products
Krojcig Mebel Sp. z o. o (51%)	Poland	Cellular polymer products
Libeltex AB	Sweden	Fibre processing
Libeltex NV	Belgium	Fibre processing
Libeltex SA	France	Fibre processing
Metzeler Mousse SA	France	Cellular polymer products
Metzeler Plastics GmbH	Germany	Polymeric products
Metzeler Schaum GmbH	Germany	Cellular polymer products
Morard Europe SA	France	Cellular polymer products
Participation Moulinage du Plouy SA	France	Fibre processing
Plastinord SA	France	Polymeric products
Poly Schaumstoffverarbeitung GmbH	Germany	Cellular polymer products
Pullflex SA	France	Cellular polymer products
Radium Foam BV	Netherlands	Cellular polymer products
Radium Latex GmbH	Germany	Cellular polymer products
Royalite Plastics SRL	Italy	Polymeric products
Tramico SA	France	Cellular polymer products

PRINCIPAL SUBSIDIARY AND ASSOCIATED UNDERTAKINGS
(continued)

Subsidiary undertakings	Country of incorporation and principal operation	Product or activities
UAB Vita Baltic International (80%)	Lithuania	Cellular polymer products
Veenendaal Schaumstoffwerk GmbH	Germany	Cellular polymer products
Vitafoam Europe BV	Netherlands	Parent company
Vita Interfoam BV	Netherlands	Parent company
Vita Polymers Denmark A/S	Denmark	Polymeric products
Vita Polymers Europe BV	Netherlands	Parent company
Vita Polymeres France SA	France	Parent company
Vita Polymers Poland Sp. z o.o.	Poland	Cellular polymer products
International		
Australia Vita Pty. Limited	Australia	Parent company
Crest Foam Industries Incorporated (80%)	USA	Cellular polymer products
RLA Polymers Pty. Limited	Australia	Polymeric compounds
Vitafoam CA (Private) Limited	Zimbabwe	Cellular polymer products
Vita Incorporated	USA	Cellular polymer products

Associated undertakings	Country of incorporation and principal operation	Issued ordinary capital Total m's	Group interest %	Results up to
United Kingdom				
BTR-Vitaline Limited	England	£0.4	50	31 Dec
Continental Europe				
Vita Cortex Holdings Limited	Ireland	IR£0.5	50	31 Dec
International				
Spartech Corporation	USA	US$17.8	33	31 Oct
Taki-Vita SAE	Egypt	E£18.0	40	31 Dec
Vitafoam Nigeria PLC	Nigeria	N72.8	20	30 Sep
Vitafoam Products Canada Limited	Canada	C$0.02	50	30 Sep

Notes:
1. Unless otherwise indicated 100% of issued share capital is owned by British Vita PLC. Interests in the Continental European and International subsidiary undertakings are held through subsidiary undertakings of British Vita PLC, the ultimate parent company.
2. The interest in BTR-Vitaline Limited is held directly by British Vita PLC. All other interests in associated undertakings are held through subsidiary undertakings of British Vita PLC.
3. The principal activity of the associated undertakings is the manufacture and processing of polymers.
4. Spartech Corporation and Vitafoam Nigeria PLC are listed, respectively, on the New York and Nigerian Stock Exchanges.
5. The accounts of all subsidiary undertakings, except Crest Foam Industries Incorporated, Participation Moulinage du Plouy SA and Vitafoam CA (Private) Limited, are audited by Arthur Andersen. The accounts of all associated undertakings, except Spartech Corporation, are audited by firms other than Arthur Andersen.

DIRECTORS' RESPONSIBILITY STATEMENT

Company law requires the directors to prepare accounts for each financial year which give a true and fair view of the state of affairs of the Company and Group and of the profit or loss of the Group for that period. In preparing those accounts, the directors are required to
■ select suitable accounting policies and then apply them consistently;
■ make judgements and estimates that are reasonable and prudent;
■ state whether applicable accounting standards have been followed, subject to any material departures disclosed and explained in the accounts; and
■ prepare the accounts on the going concern basis unless it is inappropriate to presume that the Group will continue in business.

The directors are responsible for keeping proper accounting records which disclose with reasonable accuracy at any time the financial position of the Company and Group and to enable them to ensure that the accounts comply with the Companies Act 1985. They are also responsible for safeguarding the assets of the Company and Group and hence for taking reasonable steps for the prevention and detection of fraud and other irregularities.

AUDITORS' RESPONSIBILITY STATEMENT

Company law requires auditors to form an independent opinion on the accounts presented by the directors based on their audit and to report their opinion to the shareholders. The Companies Act 1985 also requires auditors to report to the shareholders if the following requirements are not met:
■ that the companies in the Group have maintained proper accounting records;
■ that the accounts are in agreement with the accounting records;
■ that directors' emoluments and other transactions with directors are properly disclosed in the accounts; and
■ that the auditors have obtained all the information and explanations which, to the best of their knowledge and belief, are necessary for the purpose of their audit.

The auditors' opinion does not encompass the reports on pages 2 to 21. However, the Companies Act 1985 requires auditors to report to the shareholders if the matters contained in the directors' report are inconsistent with the accounts.

ARTHUR ANDERSEN

Manchester

Auditors' report to the Shareholders of British Vita PLC

We have audited the accounts on pages 24 to 44 which have been prepared under the historical cost convention, as modified by the revaluation of certain fixed assets, and the accounting policies set out on pages 22 and 23.

Respective responsibilities of directors and auditors

As described on page 45 the Company's directors are responsible for the preparation of the accounts and it is our responsibility to form an independent opinion, based on our audit, on those accounts and to report our opinion to you.

Basis of opinion

We conducted our audit in accordance with Auditing Standards issued by the Auditing Practices Board. An audit includes examination, on a test basis, of evidence relevant to the amounts and disclosures in the accounts. It also includes an assessment of the significant estimates and judgements made by the directors in the preparation of the accounts and of whether the accounting policies are appropriate to the circumstances of the Company and of the Group, consistently applied and adequately disclosed.

We planned and performed our audit so as to obtain all the information and explanations which we considered necessary in order to provide us with sufficient evidence to give reasonable assurance that the accounts are free from material misstatement, whether caused by fraud or other irregularity or error. In forming our opinion we also evaluated the overall adequacy of the presentation of information in the accounts.

Opinion

In our opinion the accounts give a true and fair view of the state of affairs of the Company and of the Group at 31 December 1997 and of the Group's profit and cash flows for the year then ended and have been properly prepared in accordance with the Companies Act 1985.

Arthur Andersen

Arthur Andersen Chartered Accountants and Registered Auditors
Bank House, 9 Charlotte Street, Manchester M1 4EU.
9 March 1998

ARTHUR ANDERSEN

Report by the Auditors to British Vita PLC on Corporate Governance Matters

In addition to our audit of the accounts, we have reviewed the directors' statements on pages 16 and 17 concerning the Company's compliance with the paragraphs of the Cadbury Code of Best Practice specified for our review by the London Stock Exchange and their adoption of the going concern basis in preparing the accounts. The objective of our review is to draw attention to non-compliance with Listing Rules 12.43(j) and 12.43(v).

We carried out our review in accordance with guidance issued by the Auditing Practices Board. That guidance does not require us to perform the additional work necessary to, and we do not, express any opinion on the effectiveness of either the Company's system of internal financial control or its corporate governance procedures nor on the ability of the Company and Group to continue in operational existence.

Opinion

With respect to the directors' statements on internal financial control on page 17 and going concern on page 16, in our opinion the directors have provided the disclosures required by the Listing Rules referred to above and such statements are not inconsistent with the information of which we are aware from our audit work on the accounts.

Based on enquiry of certain directors and officers of the Company, and examination of relevant documents, in our opinion the directors' statement on page 17 appropriately reflects the Company's compliance with the other aspects of the Code specified for our review by Listing Rule 12.43(j).

Arthur Andersen

Arthur Andersen Chartered Accountants and Registered Auditors
Bank House, 9 Charlotte Street, Manchester M1 4EU.
9 March 1998

NOTICE OF MEETING

Notice is hereby given that the Thirty-second Annual General Meeting of British Vita PLC will be held at the British Vita Training and Development Centre, Green Street, Middleton, Manchester on Wednesday 15 April 1998 at 2.30pm for the following purposes:

Ordinary business

1. To receive and consider the accounts and the reports of the directors and auditors for the year ended 31 December 1997.
2. To declare a final dividend on the Ordinary shares for the year ended 31 December 1997.
3. To re-appoint Mr R. T. Scholes as a director.
4. To re-appoint Mr M. A. Jones as a director.
5. To re-appoint Arthur Andersen as auditors of the Company and to authorise the directors to fix their remuneration.

Special business

To consider and, if thought fit, pass the following resolutions which will be proposed as ordinary or special resolutions as respectively designated:

6. Ordinary resolution
   That the rules of the Savings Related Share Option Schemes be amended to alter the definition of eligible employee to reduce the service qualification from two years to one year.
7. Ordinary resolution
   That the directors be and are hereby generally and unconditionally authorised in accordance with section 80 of the Companies Act 1985 ("the Act") to exercise all the powers of the Company to allot relevant securities (as defined in section 80(2) of the Act) of the Company on and subject to such terms as the directors may determine. The maximum aggregate nominal amount of relevant securities which may be allotted pursuant to this authority shall be £17.2m. The authority hereby conferred shall expire at the conclusion of the annual general meeting of the Company to be held in 1999 (or, if earlier, on 15 July 1999) unless renewed, varied or revoked by the Company in general meeting. The directors shall be entitled under this authority to make at any time prior to the expiry of this authority any offer or agreement which would or might require relevant securities to be allotted after the expiry of this authority. This authority shall be in substitution for and supersede and revoke any earlier such authority conferred on the directors.

8. Special resolution
   That the directors be and are hereby authorised and empowered, pursuant to section 95(1) of the Companies Act 1985 ("the Act") to allot equity securities (as defined in section 94(2) of the Act) for cash pursuant to the general authority conferred by Resolution 6 set out in the Notice convening this Meeting, as if section 89(1) of the Act did not apply to any such allotment provided that such power shall be limited to:
   (a) the allotment of equity securities in connection with a rights issue or other issue in favour of the holders of Ordinary shares where the equity securities respectively attributable to the interests of the Ordinary shareholders are proportionate (as nearly as may be) to the respective numbers of Ordinary shares held or deemed to be held by them, subject only to such exclusions or other arrangements as the directors may deem necessary or expedient to deal with fractional entitlements, legal or practical problems arising in any overseas territory or by virtue of shares being represented by depositary receipts, the requirements of any regulatory body or stock exchange, or any other matter whatsoever; and
   (b) the allotment (otherwise than pursuant to sub-paragraph (i) above) of equity securities up to an aggregate nominal value of £2.75m.
   and shall expire at the conclusion of the annual general meeting of the Company

to be held in 1999 (or, if earlier, on 15 July 1999), save that the directors may at any time prior to the expiry of this power, make any offer or agreement which would or might require equity securities to be allotted after its expiry.

By order of the Board
A. R. Teague Secretary
19 March 1998

Registered Office:
Oldham Road, Middleton,
Manchester, M24 2DB.

Notes:

1. An Ordinary shareholder entitled to attend and vote at this meeting is entitled to appoint one or more proxies to attend and, on a poll, vote instead of himself. A proxy need not be a member of the Company. Forms of proxy must reach the Company's Registrar, Lloyds Bank Registrars, by 2.30pm on Monday 13 April 1998. A form of proxy is included for the use of Ordinary shareholders. Completion and return of the proxy will not prevent an Ordinary shareholder from personally attending and voting at the meeting.

2. Copies of the amended rules of the Vita Savings Related Share Option Schemes will be available for inspection at the offices of MM&K Limited, 1 Bengal Court, Birchin Lane, London EC3V 9DD during normal office hours on any business day from the date of this notice until the close of the forthcoming Annual General Meeting.

3. Copies of the amended rules of the Vita Savings Related Share Option Schemes and the directors' contracts of service will also be available for inspection at the Registered Office of the Company during normal hours on any business day from the date of this notice until the close of the forthcoming Annual General Meeting and also at the place of that meeting for at least fifteen minutes prior to and during the meeting.

SHAREHOLDER INFORMATION

Registered office
Oldham Road
Middleton
Manchester M24 2DB
(Registered in England
and Wales No. 871669)

Auditors
Arthur Andersen
Chartered Accountants
Bank House
9 Charlotte Street
Manchester M1 4EU

Registrar and share transfer office
Lloyds Bank Registrars
The Causeway
Worthing
West Sussex
BN99 6DA
Telephone 01903 833423

Principal bankers
National Westminster Bank Plc
Lloyds Bank Plc
Deutsche Bank AG

Stockbrokers
Kleinwort Benson Securities Ltd.
Henry Cooke Lumsden Plc

Financial advisers
Kleinwort Benson Securities Ltd.

Personal Equity Plans (PEPs)
The Vita Personal Equity Plan and the Vita Single Company Personal Equity Plan enable UK residents to hold the Company's shares and receive dividends thereon free of tax. Since January 1998, both plans are operated by Bradford & Bingley (PEPs) Limited and an explanatory booklet is available from the Company or from the Bradford & Bingley helpline on 01274 555700.

Bradford & Bingley (PEPs) Limited is approved by the Inland Revenue and is regulated by PIA, the Personal Investment Authority. The tax treatment is based on the manager's understanding of the Personal Equity Plan Regulations but does not reflect the changes announced in the July and November 1997 budgets. PEPs will no longer be available from April 1999, and the tax relief on dividends will change from that date. The Government intends to launch a new form of Individual Savings Account (ISA), the exact format of which is still under discussion. It is likely that PEPs will be eligible for direct transfer into an ISA. It has been proposed that an upper limit of £50,000 should be imposed on the value of investments transferred into an ISA.

Shareholders are advised that the value of investments in the PEPs may go up or down.
Proshare
The Company is a member of Proshare, an organisation to promote wider share ownership.
Share price
During the year, the middle-market price of the Company's shares on the London Stock Exchange moved within a range from 194.5p to 260.0p, with the price on 31 December 1997 being 237.5p.

Analysis of Ordinary shareholders

Analysis by category	Numbers of shareholders	Numbers of Ordinary shares
Assurance and insurance companies	10	12,337,600
Miscellaneous bodies	397	8,354,616
Nominee companies	807	180,682,745
Private holders	2,498	18,846,896
Pension funds and pension trustees	5	1,472,093
Totals as at 9 March 1998	3,717	221,693,950

Analysis by shareholding	Numbers of shareholders	Numbers of Ordinary shares
Under 1,000	976	469,664
1,001–5,000	1,569	3,918,312
5,001–10,000	391	2,819,448
10,001–100,000	528	17,689,689
100,001–500,000	164	38,386,236
Over 500,000	89	158,410,601
Totals as at 9 March 1998	3,717	221,693,950

Financial calendar

Preliminary announcement of results for the financial year	Early March
Report and Accounts circulated	Late March
Annual General Meeting	Mid April
Interim Report	Early September
Dividend payments	
Interim	Mid November
Final	Mid May

Appendix D

Interim Report of British Vita PLC
for the Six Months Ended 30 June 1998

CHAIRMAN'S STATEMENT

A strong first-half performance with pre-tax profits of £36.8m maintaining the 15% rate of improvement over the previous year. Earnings per share increased by 14% to 10.9p and represented a 25% return on shareholders funds. These results, including sales volume growth of 9%, have been achieved against a backcloth of more difficult trading in the UK but improved market conditions in Continental Europe. Raw material prices throughout the period have, in general, remained stable.

Operating Review

The Cellular Polymers division maintained the improved margins achieved in the second-half of 1997. The UK businesses performed well against Plan and all of our Continental regions improved against the corresponding period last year. Eastern European operations in Poland achieved good results despite a slight delay in completing the new facility in Lublin. In the USA, the businesses made good progress with little overall effect in the period from the GM strike.

In the Industrial Polymers division, profits continued to grow but margins showed a slight reduction which reflects the stance taken to maintain market positions, particularly for some of our UK operations in relation to export business. The thermoplastic sheet businesses produced an excellent result relative to the same period last year, whilst compounding had mixed fortunes, with operations in Australia facing particularly difficult market conditions. Thermoplastic compounding continues to be of prime focus for development and growth, with the results showing steady progress. Our US Associate, Spartech, continued its excellent profit performance.

The Fibre operations overall had an excellent first-half with a particularly strong performance in Continental Europe. The UK produced a good result whilst the US performed satisfactorily. Our enlarged specialised yarn treatment businesses in the UK and France maintained their very strong performances. The Fabric operations showed some improvement but their overall profitability was still not satisfactory.

Portfolio Development

Our dual strategy of strongly pursuing organic growth whilst seeking value adding acquisitions resulted in the total sales volume increase of 9%, of which more than half was organic. During the first-half, two businesses joined the Industrial division at a cost of £37.6m; Axipack, a French thermoplastic sheet producer was acquired in April and Hyperlast, a leading UK producer of high performance polyurethane systems, in June.

In July an additional £41.2m was spent, for both further strengthening of our plastic compounding operations with the purchase of JGP in the North East and re-establishing our strategic level of shareholding in Spartech in the US to 44% by purchasing an additional 11% of the issued shares. Spartech continued its expansion programme with the US$135m purchase in March of Polycom Huntsman, a leading US manufacturer of polymer compounds and colour and additive concentrates.

Capital expenditure, which continues to be targeted at both organic growth and manufacturing efficiency, amounted to £18m and remained at 1.3 times depreciation.

Gearing at the half year was 6% as a result of the above acquisitions and increased further to 20% at the end of July following the Spartech/JGP deals.

Dividend

The Board has declared an interim dividend of 4.5p (4.25p) payable on 9 November 1998 to shareholders on the register at the close of business on 25 September 1998.

Recommended Offer for Doeflex Plc

We announced today a £65.9m recommended cash offer for Doeflex Plc, a major UK manufacturer of specialist plastic materials, principally compounding and sheet. Doeflex Plc represents an excellent fit within the Industrial division and provides an opportunity to further strengthen Vita's position, primarily in the UK market. An offer document will be despatched to Doeflex Plc shareholders in due course.

Year 2000

As mentioned in the latest annual Report & Accounts, considerable effort continues to be expended throughout the Group on the Year 2000 issue. Our objective is to ensure that all our companies are compliant by mid 1999 and, as a result of regular monitoring, we are satisfied with the progress being made.

Future

It is difficult to predict the impact of the turmoil that currently exists in some of the major markets of the world. The outlook for UK trading remains relatively difficult whilst Continental Europe gives more scope for optimism. Our first-half performance confirms the robustness that we have been building into Vita and we will continue to implement our strategy to develop the Group further. Product substitution for traditional materials will continue apace and Vita, with its polymer based manufacturing, is in a strong position to capitalise on this growth.

R. McGee CBE
7 September 1998

CONSOLIDATED PROFIT AND LOSS ACCOUNT
(unaudited)

			£m
Year 31 December 1997 Restated		First half 30 June 1998	1997
	Turnover		
808.4	**Continuing operations**	**418.7**	416.1
–	**Acquisitions**	**3.3**	–
808.4		**422.0**	416.1
55.5	**Operating profit – continuing operations**	**30.7**	27.0
–	**Acquisitions**	**0.4**	–
–	**Goodwill amortisation**	**(0.1)**	–
55.5		**31.0**	27.0
11.4	**Share of profits of associates – continuing operations**	**6.5**	5.6
–	**Goodwill amortisation**	**(0.1)**	–
11.4		**6.4**	5.6
66.9	**Profit before interest**	**37.4**	32.6
1.1	**Net interest receivable – Group**	**0.3**	0.4
(1.8)	**Net interest payable – Associates**	**(0.9)**	(1.0)
66.2	**Profit on ordinary activities before taxation**	**36.8**	32.0
(22.2)	**Tax on profit on ordinary activities**	**(12.4)**	(10.7)
44.0	**Profit on ordinary activities after taxation**	**24.4**	21.3
(0.2)	**Minority interests**	**(0.2)**	(0.1)
43.8	**Profit for the period**	**24.2**	21.2
(19.4)	**Dividends**	**(10.1)**	(9.4)
24.4	**Retained profit**	**14.1**	11.8
19.8p	**Earnings per Ordinary share – FRS 3**	**10.9p**	9.6p
8.75p	**Dividend per Ordinary share**	**4.5p**	4.25p

Statement of Total Recognised Gains and Losses

43.8	Profit for the period	**24.2**	21.2
(14.4)	Translation adjustments overseas net investments	**(2.8)**	(10.8)
29.4	Total recognised gains for the period	**21.4**	10.4

British Vita PLC   Interim Report 1998

GROUP BALANCE SHEET
(unaudited)

British Vita PLC   Interim Report 1998

			£m
Year 31 December 1997		First half 30 June **1998**	1997
	Fixed assets		
225.8	**Tangible assets**	**234.0**	222.4
–	**Intangible assets – goodwill**	**30.0**	–
18.8	**Investments**	**23.9**	23.9
244.6		**287.9**	246.3
	Current assets		
75.1	**Stocks**	**78.1**	76.2
161.5	**Debtors**	**172.7**	167.4
60.0	**Cash at bank and short term investments**	**40.8**	57.1
296.6		**291.6**	300.7
	Liabilities and provisions		
(52.0)	**Borrowings**	**(58.3)**	(36.4)
(183.3)	**Other creditors**	**(202.1)**	(189.6)
(18.7)	**Provisions for liabilities and charges**	**(18.7)**	(20.8)
(254.0)		**(279.1)**	(246.8)
287.2	**Net assets**	**300.4**	300.2
	Represented by:		
286.1	**Shareholders' funds**	**299.1**	299.3
1.1	**Minority interests**	**1.3**	0.9
287.2		**300.4**	300.2
129p	**Net assets per share**	**135p**	135p
(3%)	**Gearing/(Net cash)**	**6%**	(7%)
	Movements in shareholders' funds		
24.4	Retained profit	**14.1**	11.8
(14.4)	Translation adjustments overseas net investments	**(2.8)**	(10.8)
1.2	New share capital subscribed	**1.7**	0.3
(14.8)	Goodwill on acquisitions written-off	**–**	–
(8.3)	Goodwill in Spartech	**–**	–
(11.9)	Net increase (decrease)	**13.0**	1.3
298.0	Opening shareholders' funds	**286.1**	298.0
286.1	Closing shareholders' funds	**299.1**	299.3

CASH FLOW STATEMENT
(unaudited)

			£m
Year 31 December 1997		First half 30 June **1998**	1997
74.0	Net cash inflow from operating activities	**43.3**	33.0
2.9	Net cash inflow from returns on investments and servicing of finance	**2.3**	1.4
(15.6)	Taxation paid	**(4.7)**	(5.0)
(32.9)	Net cash outflow from capital expenditure	**(18.0)**	(17.6)
	Acquisitions and disposals		
(19.4)	Purchase of subsidiary undertakings	**(32.6)**	–
(0.5)	Purchase of associated undertakings	**(1.5)**	–
(19.9)	Net cash outflow from acquisitions	**(34.1)**	–
(18.8)	Equity dividends paid	**(10.0)**	(9.4)
(10.3)	Cash (outflow) inflow before use of liquid resources and financing	**(21.2)**	2.4
(9.8)	Net cash inflow (outflow) from management of liquid resources	**23.5**	(10.1)
17.3	Net cash inflow from financing	**0.9**	3.6
(2.8)	Increase (decrease) in cash in the period	**3.2**	(4.1)
	Reconciliation of net cash flow to movement in net funds:		
(2.8)	Increase (decrease) in cash in the period	**3.2**	(4.1)
(16.1)	Cash inflow (outflow) from decrease in debt and lease financing	**0.7**	(3.3)
9.8	Cash (inflow) outflow from increase in liquid resources	**(23.5)**	10.1
(9.1)	Change in debt resulting from cash flows	**(19.6)**	2.7
(0.8)	Loans and finance leases acquired with subsidiary	**(5.0)**	–
–	Finance leases	**(1.1)**	–
1.6	Translation differences	**0.2**	1.7
(8.3)	Movement in net funds in the period	**(25.5)**	4.4
16.3	Net funds at start of period	**8.0**	16.3
8.0	Net funds at end of period	**(17.5)**	20.7

SEGMENTAL ANALYSIS
(unaudited)

£m

	Turnover			Operating profit		
	First half 30 June		Year 31 Dec	First half 30 June		Year 31 Dec
	1998	1997	1997	**1998**	1997	1997
Class of business		Restated			Restated	
Cellular polymers	**233.9**	235.5	459.7	**17.5**	15.0	32.1
Industrial polymers	**112.3**	103.7	200.3	**8.6**	8.0	15.7
Fibres and fabrics	**75.8**	76.9	148.4	**4.9**	4.0	7.7
	422.0	416.1	808.4	**31.0**	27.0	55.5
Geographical origin						
United Kingdom	**176.6**	176.6	351.9	**14.7**	14.5	30.0
Continental Europe	**196.1**	193.6	362.0	**13.8**	10.6	20.8
International	**49.3**	45.9	94.5	**2.5**	1.9	4.7
	422.0	416.1	808.4	**31.0**	27.0	55.5
Geographical destination						
United Kingdom	**152.2**	152.4	303.3			
Continental Europe	**213.1**	210.6	396.4			
International	**56.7**	53.1	108.7			
	422.0	416.1	808.4			

Principal £1 equivalent exchange rates applied:

		Average			Closing		
		30.6.98	31.12.97	30.6.97	**30.6.98**	31.12.97	30.6.97
Belgium	Bfr	**61.34**	58.53	56.75	**62.06**	60.96	59.57
France	Ffr	**9.97**	9.55	9.28	**10.09**	9.90	9.73
Germany	Dm	**2.97**	2.84	2.75	**3.01**	2.96	2.89
Netherlands	Dfl	**3.35**	3.19	3.09	**3.39**	3.34	3.25
United States	$	**1.65**	1.64	1.63	**1.66**	1.65	1.66

NOTES
(unaudited)

1. Apart from the treatment of goodwill on acquisitions, the interim accounts have been prepared using accounting policies stated in the Company's Report and Accounts for the year ended 31 December 1997 and are unaudited.
   To comply with new Financial Reporting Standard, goodwill on acquisitions made during the period covered by the accounts has been capitalised and amortised over twenty years.
   The Consolidated Profit & Loss Account figures have been restated to comply with the new Financial Reporting Standard on Associates and Joint Ventures.

2. The results for the year ended 31 December 1997 are an abridged version of the Company's full accounts which carried an unqualified auditor's report and have been filed with the Registrar of Companies.

3. Taxation charge at 33.7% for the six months ended 30 June 1998 (1997 – 34%) is based on estimated effective rate of tax for the full year ending 31 December 1998.

4. Earnings per share is based on earnings (after minority interests) and on weighted average number of shares in issue, as detailed below:

	30.6.98	31.12.97	30.6.97
Earnings (£m)	24.2	43.8	21.2
Weighted average number of shares (m)	222.0	221.2	221.0

5. Net cash inflow from operating activities (£m)

	30.6.98	31.12.97	30.6.97
Operating profit	31.0	55.5	27.0
Depreciation charges	14.0	27.3	14.4
Government grants	(0.1)	(0.2)	(0.2)
Amortisation of goodwill	0.1	–	–
Loss (profit) on sale of tangible assets	0.2	(0.5)	(0.2)
Increase (decrease) in provisions	0.1	(0.7)	0.8
Increase in working capital	(2.0)	(7.4)	(8.8)
	43.3	74.0	33.0

6. Analysis of net acquisitions in the period (£m)

Tangible fixed assets	7.1
Working capital	(4.6)
Net assets acquired	
subject to borrowings	2.5
Goodwill paid	30.1
	32.6
Discharged by:	
Cash	23.7
Loan notes	8.6
Deferred consideration	0.3
	32.6

7. The comparative figures for the year ended 31 December 1997 and other financial information contained in these interim results do not constitute statutory accounts of the British Vita Group within the meaning of section 240 of the Companies Act 1985.
   Statutory accounts for the year ended 31 December 1997 have been filed with the Registrar of Companies for England and Wales and have been reported on by the British Vita Group's auditors. The report of the auditors was not qualified and did not contain a statement under section 237(2) or (3) of the Companies Act 1985.

British Vita PLC   Interim Report 1998

AUDITORS' REPORT

ARTHUR ANDERSEN

Manchester

Auditors' Review Report to British Vita PLC

We have reviewed the financial information contained in the Interim Report for the first half year ended 30 June 1998 which is the responsibility of, and has been approved by, the directors. Our responsibility is to report on the results of our review.

Our review was carried out having regard to the Bulletin 'Review of Interim Financial Information', issued by the Auditing Practice Board. This review consisted principally of applying analytical procedures to the underlying financial data, assessing whether accounting policies have been consistently applied, and making enquiries of Group Management responsible for financial and accounting matters. The review was substantially less in scope than an audit performed in accordance with Auditing Standards. Accordingly we do not express an audit opinion on the interim financial information.

On the basis of our review:

In our opinion the interim financial information has been prepared using accounting policies consistent with those adopted by British Vita PLC in its Report and Accounts for the year ended 31 December 1997, except for the changes referred to in note 1; and we are not aware of any material modifications that should be made to the interim financial information as presented.

Arthur Andersen

Arthur Andersen Chartered Accountants and Registered Auditors
Bank House, 9 Charlotte Street, Manchester M1 4EU.
7 September 1998

Index